UNLOCK
THE SECRET
MESSAGES OF
YOUR BODY!

Also by Denise Linn

Books/Oracle Cards

Altars: Bringing Sacred Shrines into Your Everyday Life

Dream Lover: Using Your Dreams to Enhance Love in Your Life

Feng Shui for the Soul: How to Create a Harmonious Environment That Will Nurture and Sustain You*

Four Acts of Personal Power: How to Heal Your Past and Create a Positive Future*

The Hidden Power of Dreams: The Mysterious World of Dreams Revealed*

If I Can Forgive, So Can You: My Autobiography of How I Overcame My Past and Healed My Life*

*Past Lives, Present Miracles: The Most Empowering Book
on Reincarnation You'll Ever Read . . . in This Lifetime!**

Quest: A Guide for Creating Your Own Vision Quest

Sacred Space: Clearing and Enhancing the Energy of Your Home

The Secret Language of Signs: How to Interpret the Coincidences and Symbols in Your Life

Secrets & Mysteries: The Glory and Pleasure of Being a Woman*

Soul Coaching®: 28 Days to Discover Your Authentic Self*

Soul Coaching® Oracle Cards: What Your Soul Wants You to Know (a 52-card deck)*

The Soul Loves the Truth: Lessons Learned on My Path to Joy*

Space Clearing: How to Purify and Create Harmony in Your Home

Space Clearing A–Z: How to Use Feng Shui to Purify and Bless Your Home*

Audio Programs

Angels! Angels! Angels!
Cellular Regeneration
Complete Relaxation*
Dreams
Journeys into Past Lives*
Life Force
Past Lives and Beyond
Phoenix Rising
The Way of the Drum

Video

Instinctive Feng Shui for Creating Sacred Space*

*Available from Hay House

⚑ ⚑ ⚑

Please visit Hay House USA: **www.hayhouse.com**®
Hay House Australia: **www.hayhouse.com**
Hay House UK: **www.hayhouse.co.uk**
Hay House South Africa: **www.hayhouse.co.za**
Hay House India: **www.hayhouse.co.in**

UNLOCK THE SECRET MESSAGES OF YOUR BODY!

A 28-Day Jump-Start Program for
Radiant Health and Glorious Vitality

Denise Linn

HAY HOUSE, INC.
Carlsbad, California • New York City
London • Sydney • Johannesburg
Vancouver • Hong Kong • New Delhi

Published and distributed in the United States by: Hay House, Inc.: www.hayhouse.com
Published and distributed in Australia by: Hay House Australia Pty. Ltd.: www.hay house.com.au • *Published and distributed in the United Kingdom by:* Hay House UK, Ltd.: www.hayhouse.co.uk • *Published and distributed in the Republic of South Africa by:* Hay House SA (Pty), Ltd.: www.hayhouse.co.za • *Distributed in Canada by:* Raincoast: www.raincoast.com • *Published in India by:* Hay House Publishers India: www.hayhouse.co.in

Editorial supervision: Jill Kramer • *Project editor:* Lisa Mitchell
Design: Julie Davison

Soul Coaching® is a registered trademark of Denise Linn Seminars, Inc.

Library of Congress Cataloging-in-Publication Data

Linn, Denise.
  Unlock the secret messages of your body! : a 28-day jump-start program for radiant health and glorious vitality / Denise Linn.
    p. cm.
  ISBN 978-1-4019-2658-8 (tradepaper : alk. paper) 1. Health. 2. Vitality. I. Title.
  RA776.L765 2010
  613--dc22

                              2009036426

ISBN: 978-1-4019-2658-8

13 12 11 10   4 3 2 1
1st edition, April 2010

Printed in the United States of America

*This book is dedicated to my husband, David;
our daughter, Meadow; our dear friend
Marika Borg; and to Allison Harter.*

Contents

CHAPTER ONE:
Air Week—Clearing Your Mental Body 1

CHAPTER TWO:
Water Week—Clearing Your Emotional Body 65

A Note from the Author

When I was 17 years old, I was attacked by an unknown gunman. As a result of that unprovoked attack, I lost numerous organs, and there was substantial damage to my body. On my journey to healing, I discovered a number of powerful techniques that dramatically improved my health. The 28-day program, outlined in this book, contains many of the life-transforming exercises that I used to experience the vibrant health I enjoy today. Additionally, thousands have used this program with profound results in their health and vitality.

What Is the Soul-Coaching Health Program?

"And the day came when the risk it took to remain tight inside the bud was more painful than the risk it took to blossom."
— **Anaïs Nin**

Do you know that there are secret messages hidden in your cells? Do you know that uncovering these messages could have a profound effect on your health, as well as every aspect of your life?

This 28-day program—which is based on my original Soul Coaching® program—takes you on a heartfelt journey into the vast inner universe of your body, where mysteries dwell as great as any that can be found in the heavenly bodies above. There are wondrous secrets in your cells, glands, and organs that can unveil countless insights about your life. As these perceptions are revealed, your radiance expands and your body becomes lighter and freer.

Your body is a receiving station that is constantly absorbing deeply meaningful messages from the world around you, as well as from spiritual spheres and your spiritual mentors. However, you can't hear those messages if your body is clogged with inner static. This interference doesn't just come from lack of exercise or an overload of junk food; in the deepest sense, it's a result of self-imposed, limiting beliefs and fears that have become lodged in your energy field.

This book will show you how to successfully maneuver through—and clear away the static from—the labyrinth of energy fields in your physical form. As you do so, your body turns into a powerful sending and receiving station of energy, light, and spirit. And, most important, you feel sparkling and bright!

The primary aim of the Soul Coaching® Health Program, outlined in the following pages, is to remove this inner debris so that you can connect with the spiritual wisdom of your body. This isn't a diet plan or a technique for controlling the intake of food and drink, nor is it a physical-exercise regimen or fitness program. There is deep intelligence in your body that absolutely knows what you need in every moment and understands that getting healthy isn't about depriving or constricting yourself. It's about living life lusciously, and cherishing and honoring yourself. This is a journey to lighten your soul and, thus, lighten your body.

Your Body Is Your Soul's Secret Messenger

In its most profound sense, the word *soul* describes your true essence. It's that place within you that is eternal and universal. It's the substance that links your body and spirit to the greater forces of the universe. When you take care of the needs of your soul, your body responds immediately. And as every cell begins to sing with joy . . . miracles abound and an inner radiance shines through you.

Every single day your soul is whispering to you; it's speaking to you through your body. If you ever want to receive an immediate message, delve deep into your body and the message will come forth. In this program, you'll learn how to listen for these insights and understand their meaning.

Mystical Synchronicities

An incredible thing happens once you commit to this program: your life will seem to unfold in a remarkable—almost magical—way. It's amazing but true! When you declare that you're ready to discover and clear any blockages within the myriad dimensions of your body (and are willing to dedicate one month of your life to doing so), then the loving forces of the universe coalesce to propel you in the direction of your destiny. Synchronistic events and seeming "coincidences" begin to increase exponentially in your life, and your life-force energy expands. I'm not sure why it happens, but I do know that it does happen.

Once you dedicate yourself to this program, the universe hears that declaration . . . and extraordinary events seem to emerge within your life, all aimed at a deep soul cleansing and clearing.

Everything That Happens Is Part of the Process
(Even If It Doesn't Seem Like It)

Once you begin, the events of your life aren't an accident. In fact, many who have engaged in this program have remarked on the astonishing synchronicities they've experienced. There are mundane coincidences— for example, during Water Week, it might rain, the plumbing might act up, or you might have bladder issues. Throughout Fire Week, you may notice electrical surges or that your body suddenly becomes very hot. There are also more profound coincidences, such as hearing from an estranged family member while you're working through the section on relationship healing. Literally, everything that happens during your 28 days is part of the process, even if it doesn't seem like it at the time.

How This Health Program Is Different from Others

This 28-day program is a powerful, *inner*-cleansing system based on three premises:

1. Everything is energy.

2. Everything is in a constant state of change.

3. Everything has consciousness.

1. *Everything is energy*—including your body—and in every moment you're influencing (and also being influenced by) a multitude of energy fields. The choices you

make, the thoughts you think, the judgments you harbor, the emotions you experience, the people you spend time with, the food you eat, the air you breathe, and the environments you occupy . . . all of these affect the energy fields that make up your body.

In this program, you'll discover what's affecting the energy fields in your body—such as the emotional clutter that manifests in physical ailments. You'll also learn what you can do to release internal mental and emotional stagnation to become more vibrant.

2. *Everything is in a constant state of change* No matter what shape your body is in, how overweight it is, or what health challenges you're facing, you *can* transform your health. Just because what you've tried before hasn't worked doesn't mean that your past needs to dictate your future. Everything changes, meaning that it's possible to heal and balance your body now . . . *even if nothing has worked to date.* Through clearing old patterns, and using your conscious intent and the law of attraction, you can change the shape and health of your body.

3. *Everything has consciousness*—every gland, organ, and cell in your body has an awareness with which you can communicate and even influence. This isn't new information; in ancient native cultures, interfacing with the body on a cellular level was considered a pathway to healing.

In an even deeper sense, your personal consciousness isn't separate from the consciousness of the universe. To the extent that you can discover the intimate connection between yourself and the world around you, the more you can transform your body. In other words, the more you can feel "at home" in the world—no matter where you are or who you're with—the more you'll feel at home in your body, and vice versa.

The Soul (and the Body) Loves the Truth

This 28-day program is about unlocking the secret messages within, revealing the truth about your life and your body. When you tell the truth, your energy, vibrancy, and health increases. When you don't, you become depleted and your body suffers. Many people are exhausted, out of shape, overweight, or in poor health because they're not being starkly honest with themselves. *When you are authentic, your soul and body thrive.*

Just because—under normal circumstances in life—you tell the truth, this doesn't mean that you're not lying about your life. Many individuals don't even realize they're being dishonest with themselves. The hardest untruths to shatter are the ones that you've been holding on to for so long that you've come to believe they're true. For example, some people put forth tremendous effort in convincing themselves that they love their job, even when their body (which is the soul's messenger) sends communications by becoming lethargic, tired, and dull only at work. It's as if the body were saying, "Hey, dude! This isn't working!" Those who ignore these messages and continue to assume that all is well may find that their body becomes increasingly depleted.

This 28-day program is about uncovering the reality of who you are and what you're really feeling, which will have a profound effect on your health. When you live and act in accordance with the dictates and truths of your soul, your body flourishes.

Your Body as Your Oracle

You'll also discover, in the next four weeks, the ways in which your body can be a powerful oracle. You'll learn how to ask a question and receive the answer. The bodily sensations you experience upon asking the question (and where they occur, specifically) can offer you direct answers from your soul. During this program, you'll also have the opportunity to uncover exactly what you need for your optimum health.

Call Upon Spiritual Guidance

Of course, you can do this program on your own . . . and you'll get results. However, if you're willing to call upon your spiritual helpers, angels, guides, ancestors, allies, and soul guardians for assistance, the results will be much more enlightening. Simply taking the time—every day during this program—to ask for guidance and support will magnify everything you achieve. Your prayers don't need to be elaborate or long. In fact, a prayer or request in straightforward, simple language will go a lot further than something that's overly complicated or lengthy.

Incorporating the Four Elements

This 28-day Soul-Coaching® Health Program is a spiritual journey that's also divided into four one-week periods. Each week is dedicated to one of the four elements: Air, Water, Fire, and Earth. In a mysterious and organic way, our memories, beliefs, and emotions are tied to the elements of nature. By activating these elements within us, we also activate quadrants of our souls. This in turn has a potent effect on our bodies.

Throughout history, these elements have been associated with the mental, emotional, spiritual, and physical parts of ourselves. They've been associated with natural balance and wholeness. Ancient native people knew that within each element were patterns of energy that permeated the universe. Hippocrates, honored as the father of modern medicine, declared that *a patient's health depended upon a balance of these four elements.* The great Sufi poet Rumi wrote that the four elements were the foundation of life and deeply impacted the human spirit. In the mystery schools of Mesopotamia, initiates underwent rigorous rites of Air, Water, Fire, and Earth. Each elemental rite was said to test a particular aspect of the initiate's nature. From Native Americans to ancient Greeks, Egyptians, Mayans, Aztecs, Persians, Celts, and Hindus, the enigmatic panorama of nature has been divided into these four separate parts to facilitate health and balance.

When you embark on this program, it's valuable to do it in the context of the cycles of nature and the elements of Air, Water, Fire, and Earth, which will reconnect you to your ancient roots.

An Overview of the Soul-Coaching Health Program

Here's a quick breakdown of each week of the program; and in the next few pages, I'll answer the most common questions and concerns that I've encountered from people who've embarked on this soul journey with me.

- *Days 1–7* are devoted to the properties of Air and are focused on clearing your mental body.

- *Days 8–14* are devoted to the properties of Water and are focused on clearing your emotional body.

- *Days 15–21* are devoted to the properties of Fire and are focused on clearing the shadows to connect with your spiritual body.

- *Days 22–28* are devoted to the properties of Earth and are focused on clearing and strengthening your physical body.

How Can I Fit This Program into My Busy Life?

You absolutely can do this program, no matter how busy you are or how hectic your life is. It's designed so that anyone can complete it. There are assignments for each day that are divided into three levels, and you choose the level that's appropriate for you for that day. Regardless of which level you choose, you'll achieve results.

Level 1: *Committed to Change!* Usually takes 5 to 15 minutes per day.

Level 2: *Going for It!* Includes the Level 1 exercises and usually takes 10 to 30 minutes per day.

Level 3: *Playing Full Out!* Includes the Level 1 and Level 2 exercises and takes as long as is necessary. (It could last anywhere from half an hour to several hours, depending on the exercise.)

Some days you may just want to participate at the "Committed to Change!" level, and there may be other days when you want to "Play Full Out!" You may wish to select a level of participation for the whole 28-day process, or you can decide to vary the levels as you see fit. Do what works for you.

When Should I Start This Program?

You may choose to begin on the first day of the month, or follow the 28-day moon cycle, starting with either the full or new moon. You can initiate this program at the winter or summer solstice or in early spring—a time of new beginnings. Alternatively, you may want to schedule this during your vacation, or perhaps kick it off on January 1. Or maybe you'd like to start today! *The most important thing is that you begin.* Often when people wait for the perfect time, opportunity passes them by. When you plunge in (even if the timing doesn't seem ideal), dramatic results are often produced.

Since the 28 days are divided into four elemental cycles, you can also do this over a four-month period or even extend it over the course of a year assigning one elemental cycle to each season. You can also do this program in 28 weeks, by doing each assignment over the course of a week rather than a day. However, it's easy to lose steam if you take a long time—that's why I've designed the program to be completed in 28 days.

Should I Do This Alone or with Others?

Although many do this on their own with remarkable success, it's often easier to complete any kind of health program if you have a group of people sharing the experience with you. The support and encouragement of others can be motivating.

You might consider gathering a group of friends to do the program together. Meet once a week to compare progress. Every time someone has a "health win," celebrate like crazy. For example, when Joan started the program, she couldn't get to the top of the stairs without stopping to catch her breath. Two weeks in, however, she could sail up the steps! Her group threw a celebration in her honor, complete with balloons. That support spurred her on to achieve even more positive results. Some groups choose to meet once a week for 28 weeks, dedicating one week per assignment. Another idea is to form an online group, so you can support each other via daily e-mails. Thousands of people have participated in Soul Coaching online with excellent results.

You can also log on to **www.DeniseLinn.com** or **www.Soul-Coaching.com** to locate a certified Soul Coach™ in your area. (These are highly qualified individuals whom I have personally trained in my methods.) When you work with a Soul Coach, you have someone who can guide you one step at a time through the program.

My Letters to You

When I created this health program, I guided a group through it online. I sent a daily message with an introduction to that day's exercises. The feedback about my letters was so encouraging that I decided to include them in this book. As you read my letter at the beginning of each day's exercises, imagine that—through these words—I am personally supporting you on your health journey.

Shouldn't a Health Program Take Longer Than 28 Days?

Jump-start is the key word here. Your health is a life-long quest, but sometimes to change the course of your life, you need to jump-start that change. This is especially important when a person's identity is tied into less-than-perfect health. For example, maybe you subconsciously believe that you *are* "a person who's out of shape" or "an overweight person." It's part of your identity. This program is meant to get things rolling to change the damaging perceptions of who you are and what you can accomplish. Once you've begun to transform those old beliefs, it's so much easier to heal your body. The impetus you gain on this jump-start program can carry you forward into the rest of your healthy and vibrant life.

What If I Can't Seem to Stick to Any Program?

Of course you already know what you need to do to get healthy. Almost everyone who watches television, listens to the radio, or reads newspapers or magazines knows what their health problems are . . . and what they can do about them. You're aware of the potentially dire consequences if you *don't* change your life, but either you don't (or can't) seem able to take action. Or if you do start to make positive changes, you end up sabotaging your efforts to become healthier.

I carry extra weight on my body—it may always be like that. I'm a luscious, big woman; I may never be a "skinny chick." And in the past when I tried to get fit, something seemed to sabotage my efforts. (If you're like me, whenever you attempt something like this, it seems as if there's another part of you that rebels.) When I tried to drop some weight, it felt like an authority figure popped up and was commanding me in a stern voice: "You have to reduce the amount you're eating! You need to exercise now!"

Then a raging sub-personality within me would roar forward: "How dare you tell me what to do! I will *not* be bullied by you! I'm going to show you—I'm going to eat all I want!" And then I'd eat more before noon than I usually ate in two days, filled with the grim satisfaction that no one could tell me what to do. It didn't matter that *I* was the one who wanted to get healthy in the first place; there would be a deeper part of me that rebelled.

There are three parts of the brain: the *conscious* brain, called the neocortex, which controls reasoning and language; the more primitive *limbic* brain that controls a person's emotional response to life; and the *reptilian* brain. This third part controls the body's vital functions such as breathing and heart rate. But it's the limbic brain that often sabotages your pursuit of health. If you consciously desire to take steps toward greater health, but your yearning is at cross-purposes with your limbic brain, this more primal part of you will have much more potent control of your actions. This is the reason why it's hard to stick to any health program. If you consciously desire change, but it's at odds with the dictates of your limbic brain, guess who always wins?

Don't Wake the Dragon—Be Gentle with Yourself

The limbic brain—which developed roughly 150 million years ago—has ancestral cellular memories of past times of starvation, "fight or flight," and of the struggle to survive. If your conscious-reasoning mind—which only evolved about two or three million years ago—has a plan or desire that the older, more primitive limbic brain feels threatened by, it will rear its head and command control of the situation. It's as if there's a sleeping dragon inside of you that can charge forward at any time and sabotage your plans.

During the next 28 days, you're going to find ways to tiptoe around your sleeping dragon so that he doesn't wake up . . . allowing you to take control of your destiny. One method to achieve this is to be very gentle with yourself when you do these exercises for the next four weeks. *You don't have to be perfect for this program to work miracles in your life.* It's not a competition, school assignment, or a contest. It works—in a remarkable way—in spite of your sometimes feeling that you aren't doing it right.

Forgive yourself when you don't do every exercise exactly as described. Do the best you can. Almost everyone who has done the program has mentioned that even though they missed an exercise, or didn't fully do it, *they still had amazing results.*

Fall Down Seven . . . Get Up Eight

This is a Japanese expression that I love: *Fall down seven, get up eight.* It means that even if you fail several times, do *not* stay down—you're not a failure if you fall down, only if you stay down. Get up and try again.

So what if the dragon wakes up and you lose a battle or two? If you loaded up on a bag of candy bars one day, well . . . he won that battle. Tip your hat to him and just keep going. You might want to keep score (Dragon: 2, Me: 4). Don't quit . . . just forge ahead, and eventually that scorecard will balance in your favor.

Remember that the goal of this program is an activation of health and vitality. It's *not* about doing the program perfectly . . . *it's about results.* In other words, in this program, focus on your accomplishments, not on what you didn't complete. Have trust that changes are occurring at a deep level even if you don't do the program perfectly.

I tend to be the kind of person who starts a program and then when I don't do it flawlessly (like on the first day), I throw my hands up in the air and say, "That's it! I failed. It's not working. I have to start over again."

Does that sound familiar? This program is different. It works even when you mess up. It really works! You just have to keep going . . . no matter what. Even if you dedicate less than a minute a day to it, keep going. Celebrate what you *did* complete, and let go of what you didn't.

You Don't Have to Do It Perfectly . . . It Works Anyway!

Many years ago, I was asked by a publisher to write my first book. I was paralyzed with fear. Who was *I* to write a book? I thought that I didn't know enough. I figured I wasn't smart enough, and I was sure that I wasn't credible enough. I convinced myself that *I* wasn't enough. Finally, I went to see a counselor to help me work through these issues so I could write the book, and she shared something profound with me: "It doesn't have to be perfect, but it does have to get done."

Armed with this information, I proceeded to write an "imperfect" book and told myself that it was okay if it didn't meet my expectations, but I had to get it done. The astounding thing is that this book (*The Hidden Power of Dreams*) is still in print and has received many accolades over the years, but it never would have been published if I had remained hung up on perfection.

When you start this program, be willing to do it in whatever way you can. Don't judge yourself for what you *don't* do, but celebrate absolutely everything that you *do* complete. And keep going! *It doesn't have to be perfect . . . but it does have to be done.*

Facing Your Fears

Facing your fears is one way to overcome them, and one path to success with this program is to confront why you think it might not succeed. Here's an exercise that can help: Write down all of the reasons why you might think this program *won't* work for you. For example, maybe you've attempted lots of health programs, weight-management diets, strength-building systems . . . and nothing has ever worked, so you assume that this Soul Coaching program probably won't either. Here are some examples of thoughts you may be harboring:

- *I'm just too busy to do this program with any consistency, so it probably won't work.*

- *I just want to learn a few new techniques, but I don't really expect any personal results.*

- *I always sabotage every attempt to empower myself / drop weight / stay focused / keep my health commitments, so this probably won't work either.*

- *I have no self-discipline, and a program can't work without it.*

- *My health isn't really that bad. Lots of people are much worse off than I am.*

- *The temptation to "fall off the wagon" is too strong since everyone around me has poor health habits.*

Write as many as you can . . . even the ones that seem unreasonable yet still linger in some dark crevice in your mind.

Now look at your list. Take a big black marker and forcefully cross everything out, shouting out loud (or in your head): "Bulls--t!" (Or something equally dramatic.)

By doing this exercise, you've allowed yourself to:

1. Acknowledge the reasons why you feel that you won't succeed—this step brings these thoughts to the surface to be dispersed.

2. Take a forceful stand to be in control of your own destiny by making your declaration out loud.

Kick the Gnomes Out of Bed—Release Limiting Beliefs

It's absolutely true that if you eat in a healthy way and exercise regularly, you'll get in shape. But in order to become incredibly healthy on a *permanent basis,* it's essential that you shift any limiting inner thoughts about who you are and what you deserve. Until you accept your full majesty and begin to release any negative beliefs about yourself and your body, your subconscious mind may continue to sabotage any attempt you make to be as radiant as you can be.

This program will show you how to confront those nagging thoughts that seem to stand in your way. During the next 28 days, there may be times when you feel discouraged or frustrated that it's not going exactly the way you'd hoped. Or there might be times that you find yourself struggling to complete the exercises . . . and judging yourself for not doing it better or doubting your own abilities and capabilities.

These kinds of thoughts are like gnarly gnomes with their pickaxes, hacking away at your equilibrium. You know those gremlin-like critters. They live deep inside of you; and when you want to take a risk, try something new, or change your life, they start hammering away at your self-confidence.

In my own life, these self-deprecating thoughts occur frequently when I first wake up in the morning (which is probably why I try to jump out of bed rather than luxuriate under the covers). On the occasions when I do linger in bed, I often feel like I'm doing battle with these irritating beings. To rid myself of negative thoughts, I visualize kicking them out of my bed and telling them that they have no place here.

Name Your Gnomes—Give Form to the Formless

Giving a face and form to these kinds of thoughts makes it easier to dispel them. For example, I have one droopy, downtrodden gnome—I call him Mr. Sniveler—who whines: "Nothing is ever going to change, Denise, no matter how hard you try. Everything is always going to stay the same. You'll never succeed. You're a failure."

Another one is a very skinny gnome who's always dashing around and nervously looking over her shoulder. Mrs. Frenetic's rant is usually something like: "You've got too much to do! You can't possibly rest until it's all done . . . but it will *never* be done. You don't have time to spare!"

Mr. Stagnant is a worrisome, overweight, waddling gnome who usually just says, "You're ugly. You're fat. You're old. It's only going to get worse. And it's all your fault because you don't have any self-discipline."

It doesn't matter that what they say isn't true; it can still drag me down. It's negative mind chatter that needs to be dispelled. When these gnomes (and all their cousins) start niggling at my mind, I imagine giving them each a good thump as I kick them out of bed and proceed to get on with my life.

The instant you give form to your fears and worries (rather than having nebulous, unconscious concerns), you begin to move toward having control over them.

Get Juiced (with Joy)

When your cells are radiating with joy, your entire immune system responds powerfully and instantly. More than diet and exercise, this emotion illuminates and juices your cells. When you step into extraordinary happiness, every cell in your body responds. It's one of the fastest ways to empower and strengthen your body. Over 30 studies have indicated that being happy can protect you from getting ill. In fact, the effect of joy on your life span is as strong as the effect of not smoking. It's kind of a fountain of youth.

You don't attract what you want; you attract what you are. If you want great health, but your vibratory rate is low and you're feeling pessimistic about life, chances are it's not going to happen easily. But if you're radiating delight and optimism, your health will respond with shimmering vibrancy.

During the next 28 days, find as much joy as you can . . . daily, hourly, and in every minute. As much as possible, become a beacon of bliss. Live in the ecstatic state of gratitude. The more you're grateful for what you have (instead of complaining or being frustrated), the more your health expands.

Become a Beacon of Bliss

If you turn this program into a duty or discipline, it can work—that's true. But if you make it joyous, lighthearted, and a delight to wake up to see what you're going to uncover about yourself or what obstacles to your health you're going to release, then your results will be greatly magnified. Here are some things you can do to become a "beacon of bliss."

Pick Your Theme Song

Have you ever noticed how a song can magically ignite a particular feeling in you? One way to increase pleasure while working through this program is to pick a theme song for the month . . . and play it every day. Your theme song is like a sound track for your life while traveling along the 28 days, magnifying everything you do on your journey. If you use a song that always inspires you or makes you feel happy and energized, it will be much easier to persevere.

So before starting, focus on finding a song that *juices* you. Choose one that gives you a feeling of vitality and vigor. In other words, don't pick the song that you played a zillion times during a breakup that makes you sad every time you hear it!

Shake Your Booty

Another way to exalt your month is to move your body/dance/wiggle to your theme song. Think you don't have time? There's *always* time to move your body. Just imagine your song in your mind, and bop down the aisles at the grocery store to the music playing through the store speakers. Silly? Embarrassing? Sure it is. Absolutely. But if you want to shift where you are, you need to start doing things in a different way. You know that old expression: If you do what you've always done, you'll get what you've always gotten.

Create a Slogan

Slogans work. That's why all great marketing campaigns use them. They're an effective way of programming you to buy certain products. And if they work for advertisers, they can work for you to reinforce what you do on this program. Come up with a slogan for your-self for the month. It doesn't have to be original. How about any of the following: "Just do it!" "When the going gets tough, the tough get going!" or (if you have a life-threatening disease like cancer) "Game on, Cancer! You're going down!"

Your slogan doesn't even have to make sense; it could be something like: "Life rocks!" or "Shazam!" The important thing is that every time you say it, you feel strong and ready to pick yourself up and keep going.

Give Yourself a Secret Power Name

During the next 28 days, choose a secret power name for yourself. I have a friend, for example, who calls herself "Cardio Queen." Every time she declares "I am Cardio Queen!" to herself, she describes the feeling as taking off like a speeding bullet, which inspires her to move, dance, and exercise.

In mystical traditions, you'd have an everyday name that people called you, and you'd also have a power name. It was believed that with it, you could tap into a source of strength that could enhance your life. My power name is "Panther Dancer"; and every time I think of myself as Panther Dancer, I feel sleek, powerful, and supple. It reinforces this feeling within myself and helps me create an identity that's vital and healthy.

Rewards, Prizes, and Joyous Pleasures!

It's the human condition to avoid discomfort at any cost; we're wired to steer clear of pain and seek out pleasure. So in this program, I've included a way to bring you immense joy: there are incentives! Not only will you achieve dramatic results in your body, but there are also prizes along the way. I call this aspect of the program "rewards, prizes, and joyous pleasures."

Here's how it works: Every time you complete a step, you can give yourself your self-prescribed reward for that day. You don't have to complete all three levels to achieve it . . . *any* level that you do entitles you to this. Some examples of daily rewards might be reading a good book with a cup of tea, taking a walk in the park, buying a new lipstick or a magazine, spending time with a good friend, kicking back with your feet up, dancing to your favorite songs, or whatever else you might enjoy!

If you successfully complete a week—in other words, you've completed at least one level for seven days in a row—you get an even bigger self-prescribed prize. Some examples of end-of-the-week rewards might be a night out at the movies, a get-together with friends, an afternoon at the beach or a museum, or another one of your favorite activities.

As a suggestion, go through the program now; and write out the rewards, prizes, or pleasures that you'll gift yourself for each day and week completed. There's space to jot down your reward at the beginning of each day's entry and at the end of each week (you could also write this down in your journal). And to celebrate the completion of the program, you might consider planning a memorable outing or getting yourself a special gift and wrapping it in beautiful paper to open on the last day of the program.

Listen to Your Soul, and Write Down the Messages You Receive!

Set a few moments of quiet time aside in the morning and evening to ask your body if there's anything you need to know or if it would like to communicate a message to you regarding your health or your life. *This may be the single most important thing you do each day.* This specific act of intent can open your ability to be receptive to your inner wisdom. After you receive your message for the day, you might consider writing it down in a journal.

Since the first time a caveman discovered that he could chronicle the events of his life with a charred stick on a stone wall, humans have been recording the experiences of their lives. Even in ancient times, people experienced the value of doing this. They understood that the written word has the power to transform lives.

You can look at your options, determine your goals, release blocked emotions, reframe the past, and even gain spiritual insights simply by writing in a journal. Your body can actually become much healthier if you take some time to jot down your thoughts and feelings. All you need is some paper and a pen and the willingness to tell the truth to yourself in written form.

Interestingly, researchers at the University of Texas have discovered what journal writers have always known: *journal writing is good for your health!* The authors of the study found that people who wrote about their deepest thoughts, especially about upsetting or traumatic events, *visited their doctor half as much* as those who didn't keep a journal. Journal writers also have a stronger immune system.

Additional research at the University of New York at Stony Brook monitored 112 patients who had either arthritis or asthma. The subjects were asked to write about a stressful event in their life in a journal for 20 minutes, three days a week. Of the group who expressed their feelings via their journal, *50 percent showed a dramatic improvement in their disease after only four months.* Study after study has confirmed these findings. Once you've written it down in your journal, you no longer carry much of the experience inside of you. It's on the paper and out of your body.

Your Process Journal and Joy Journal

Keep two journals during the program. The first is your *Process Journal,* which is meant for mental and emotional clearing. In it, you'll express your feelings and keep track of the insights incurred as a result of the daily assignments. It doesn't need to be neat and tidy—messy is fine! Sentences don't have to be perfectly constructed. Your Process Journal is a safe place where you can be starkly honest and record your thoughts in any way you desire.

Your *Joy Journal* is where you write about what brought you joy during each day. You might include creative writing, collages, drawings, poetry, or photos to chronicle these splendid moments. Add an entry each day—for 28 days—to describe your experiences and observations throughout the program. Even when you face challenges, there are always special moments. Record them in a way that brings you joy.

Fire Up Your Progress with Daily Affirmations

An affirmation is a positive statement that a person writes down (or recites aloud or silently) in order to counteract negative beliefs. As children, and all throughout life, we often accept limitations about ourselves . . . and then we subconsciously repeat them, over and over in our internal conversations until they seem real. These "beliefs" eventually become self-fulfilling prophecies because we're drawn to people and situations that validate our deepest inner beliefs.

One way to change your health is to change the negative thoughts you have about your body, and affirmations can help you achieve this. Your word is your wand. If you constantly say to yourself, *I'm not good enough,* your subconscious mind begins to believe it, and then you feel and act "not good enough." Consequently, people will treat you in a demeaning way, and your body's immune system will become diminished as your self-esteem plummets.

Every day during this program, you'll be given a carefully chosen affirmation that's appropriate to the assignments. These positive statements will help you create a new destiny for your health and well-being. Some people prefer to write them down on Post-its and put them on their computer, mirror, or refrigerator as a periodic reminder. Alternatively, you can repeat the affirmation to yourself throughout the day.

This Program Is <u>Not</u> about Willpower

If it took willpower to make this program succeed, it's virtually a certainty that you'd become more out of shape, fatter, or flabbier in the long run. Willpower simply doesn't work. It takes time for caterpillars to turn into butterflies, and it's going to take patience and perseverance to retrain your mind and break old habits, but you can (and will!) get there naturally and easily.

The Wild, Crazy Detox Phenomenon

It's not uncommon for those who start any kind of self-exploration program to experience a kind of detoxification that seems to arrive spontaneously. It's almost as if the soul recognizes that it's *not* life as usual; it knows that this is an opportunity to release old, negative patterns. So instead of keeping them buried deep in your psyche, your soul yanks them out, letting them float to the surface of your consciousness. In this way, you have the chance to examine and relinquish those limiting beliefs.

Don't be surprised if an old pattern rears its head while you're working through the program. It's like cream coming to the surface so that it can be skimmed off. During the next four weeks, numerous limiting patterns will be "skimmed" from your energy fields. Also know that it isn't uncommon for prior health symptoms or past ailments to arise. After all, you're literally detoxifying your body and soul. Hang in there if this happens to you!

What Is Your Comfort Zone?

One reason why it's sometimes difficult to step into more vibrant health is because we each have a comfort zone regarding our well-being. Even if we feel discomfort or pain, if we subconsciously believe that this is who we are—in other words, if that's our comfort zone—it will be almost impossible to change.

In a mysterious way, our identity is actually tied into our health issues. *One of the most potent forces of a human being is the need to stay consistent with his or her identity.* For example, Ruth had terrible joint pain. Her three close friends also experienced joint pain, and the bulk of their time spent together consisted of talking about their aches. Interestingly, it provided Ruth with a sense of comfort, knowing that her friends were dealing with the same issue. Even though she hated the pain, her identity was someone who had throbbing joints.

During her journey through the 28-day program, Ruth had the opportunity to go deep into her suffering. One of the things she discovered was that a part of her didn't want to heal because she was afraid it would mean that she'd lose her friends. She subconsciously worried that they'd feel threatened by the fact that she didn't have any more pain. This was a valuable insight for Ruth, because she was then able to create a strategy so that her joints could heal and she could still maintain her friendships.

As strange as it might sound, some people who really want to lose weight will become increasingly ill at ease when they start dropping pounds because they're moving beyond their comfort zone. Their self-image is of someone who is overweight, and when that starts to change, it can feel like a death of sorts. In fact, it *is* a death of that part of their identity, so it can feel threatening when their body begins to change. There's even a sense of internal grieving at the loss of the weight.

Other people say that they really want to diminish the constant stress in their life, yet when they truly start to relax, that can create its own kind of anxiety, anger, or disorientation because it feels so foreign. In a peculiar way, the stress is uncomfortable . . . but it's familiar. So when these individuals make changes to decrease stress, a part of them actually feels threatened.

In this program, you'll have ample opportunities to gain a clear picture of *your* comfort zone. And through this perception and other insights, you'll discern whether your identity is tied to any of your health challenges and what you can do to change this.

Make a Sacred Contract with Yourself

Create a contract for yourself that clearly states your intention for the next 28 days, and then sign it. Giving your word—and sticking to it—is important. Many people are often meticulous in keeping promises to others, yet they'll easily break a commitment to themselves. However, the vows you make to yourself are even more important to the soul than the ones you make to others. If someone continually broke his or her word, after a while you'd think that the person was untrustworthy. When you repeatedly break your word with yourself, it's a message to your subconscious mind that you aren't trustworthy or valued, and often your self-esteem and health suffer. For this program, your commitment to yourself is as sacrosanct as if you'd made a solemn promise to a cherished friend.

You can make your sacred contract as specific or as general as you like. Use words that work for you, and create honest and realistic goals. Be sure to write it down on paper, sign it, and add the date. You might even want to post it in a prominent spot in your home, or put it at the beginning of your Process Journal.

Create an Altar

An altar can be a powerful way to magnify the energy you generate on this program. It doesn't need to have religious meaning or overtones; rather, it can be a highly personal representation of what is most important to you and what you hold sacred. Even if you don't spend time in meditation at your altar, simply having one dedicated to your health is a powerful subliminal reminder that can deepen the results you attain.

To make your altar, all you need is a table or shelf. Spread a beautiful cloth on the surface, and then place things on it that represent your intention for your "Soul Full" journey for the next 28 days. Your altar should hold items that create the feeling of sparkling health.

Things Aren't Always as They Seem

Even when you think that nothing is happening (or you feel that you could be doing the program better), *things aren't always as they seem.* Beneath the surface of your consciousness, profound changes are occurring in accordance with your highest good. Your conscious mind is often the last to know what's going on. Believe and trust. You wouldn't plant seeds in your garden one afternoon and then go out the next morning and start screaming, "Where are my tomatoes?!"

Just because you can't immediately see the fruits of your labor, it doesn't mean that something powerful isn't occurring beneath the surface. *Please don't yell at your seeds, and whatever you do, don't dig them up!*

The Universe Is Open for Business . . . Place Your Order

During this program, you're going to maintain a clear focus on your health goals. Think of it as placing your order with the universe. *Where intention goes, energy flows.* Taking time to clarify your intention before you start will help determine the form that your program takes during the 28 days. Answering the following questions can be helpful:

- *Why am I doing this program?*
- *What end results do I desire?*
- *Am I really ready to make changes in my life?*

Enjoy the coming month. Remember to be gentle with yourself, and cherish your accomplishments. Feel free to go through the program in whatever way works best for you. Don't wait for the perfect time to start—the fact that you've read this far has already initiated your steps toward your sparkling light, joy, and vitality.

You are now ready to begin your spiritual journey into the vast inner wonders of your body, activating your radiant life force.

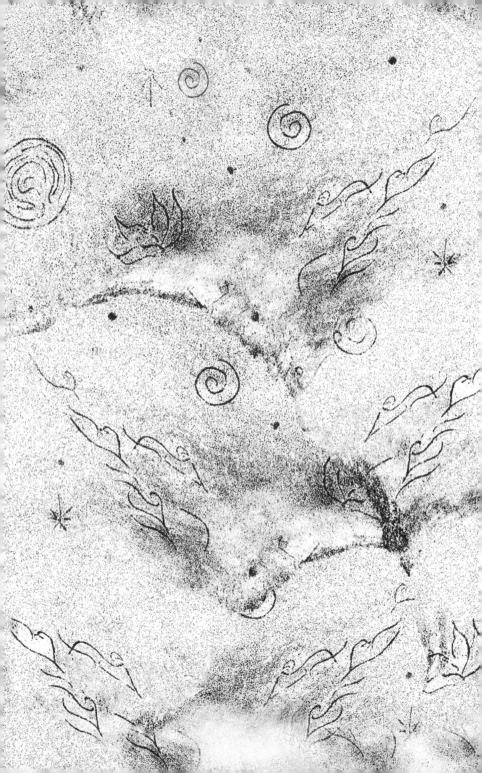

CHAPTER ONE

Air Week—Clearing Your Mental Body

I love to stand on top of the hill at Summerhill Ranch (where I live on the central coast of California with my husband, David, and our menagerie of animals) and throw my arms high over my head as I inhale the sweet air. I breathe in the Pacific Ocean breezes that make their way to us over the Santa Lucia Mountains. As I inhale, I imagine that I'm breathing in the deep souls of the ancient oaks that dot the land and drawing in the musky essence of the vineyards that surround our home. With every breath, the mental cobwebs of my being are cleared away.

The first seven days of this program are dedicated to mental clearing. As you examine this part of yourself, your body will respond in positive and powerful ways. During this week, you'll embrace the Spirit of Air that represents the aspect of self as well as mental clarity, assessment, discernment, analytical thinking, beliefs, evaluation, judgment, perception, and communication. The Air element also allows you to see situations from a higher perspective. Every exercise is aimed at clearing mental blockages to gaining vibrant health, while at the same time oxygenating your body.

Although seemingly subtle and unseen, the air allows a constant communion with the entire planet. With every breath you take, you're inhaling air that has been in every crevice of the world, from the dry region of the Sahara, to the heights of the Himalayas, to the lush and humid Amazon rain forest. The breath you just took contained at least 400,000 of the same argon atoms that Socrates inhaled throughout his life! The air that you're breathing now has been in me, and the breath that I'm inhaling right now has been in you. Thus, aligning to the Spirit of Air is a powerful way to deeply connect with the inner and outer world. It's no wonder why yogis, mystics, and sages emphasize the power of breath for spiritual practices.

1. Clearing Mental Blockages to Excellent Health

In the first seven days of the program, you'll focus on clearing mental blockages and barriers that hinder your well-being. You'll also conduct a health assessment and an inner and outer clutter-clearing. Don't be concerned if "air" (or mental) challenges come your way this week—this isn't uncommon. For example, sometimes during Air Week you might become even more aware of your lungs. Likewise, you may find yourself buffeted by strong winds (literally or symbolically), there might be issues with air-conditioning units or fans, or you could encounter problems that require your mental assessment.

Use these challenges as opportunities to clear out what you no longer need in your life. In the deeper realms, the energy of Air Week will begin to rejuvenate your brain, enhancing mental capacity and clarity and improving your memory.

2. Breathe! Oxygenating Your Body

If you could choose only one thing to do for your health, it should be to learn to breathe deeply and fully. During this week, focus on your breath. Fill your lungs as much as possible, then exhale as if you're releasing air from a balloon. Pick a time—every day—to relax and become aware of the air that enters and leaves your body. Observe your breath. Is it shallow or deep? Do you periodically hold your breath? Where is your breath concentrated? In the abdomen? In the chest area?

As you do so, you're oxygenating your body and filling every cell and crevice with the healing power of air. It's been hypothesized that the heart doesn't get cancer because of the stream of oxygen that flows through it on a daily basis. *The more you oxygenate your body, the healthier you will be.*

3. Expanding Your Awareness of the Air Around You

Throughout this week, focus your awareness and attention on the air that surrounds you. One of the most direct and powerful ways to connect with the Spirit of Air is through the breezes, which continually blow across the planet. When you go outdoors, notice the movement of air across your skin. Did you know that many native people believe that the wind carries messages from the sacred realms? Listen to the stillness in the air when you leave your house in the morning. (Yes, there are messages even when the air seems motionless.) Smell the air and sense where it has been. Be sure to open your windows and allow the air to circulate throughout your home. It will quickly clear out any stagnant energy.

In addition, imagine how it would feel to *be* a gentle spring breeze, a canyon wind, a gusty gale, rising currents, and even still air. Note any memories or messages that float into your consciousness. Just view these in the way in which you'd gaze at clouds floating overhead on a warm summer afternoon. When you're finished, write down all of your feelings and observations in your Process Journal.

4. Activating Inspiration

The Air element is also associated with inspiration, and this can take the form of what you read, what you think about, and even what you listen to (sound travels though the air). Numerous studies have shown a correlation in what you focus on and your health. During this week, I suggest that you read inspirational books or poetry (or health books that are motivating). As you do so, your immune system will strengthen.

Research has also found a dramatic relationship between music and health. So during Air Week, be sure to listen to relaxing or uplifting music. You may also want to consider going on a "media" cleanse (cut back on television, radio, the Internet, and newspapers) so that you're not filling your mind with an overabundance of negative messages and images.

Remember to write down what's great about each day in your Joy Journal. The more you focus on the wonderful and splendid moments in your life, the more balanced and beautiful your life will become.

During Air Week

- Assess and evaluate your health.

- Make a commitment to your body.

- Examine your core beliefs and inner rules regarding your health.

- Clear your clutter.

- Do the things that you've been putting off regarding your health.

- Cut back on media exposure.

- Breathe and become aware of your breathing patterns.

- Notice sounds in your environment, and listen to inspiring music.

- Communicate your truth.

✤ ✤ ✤

Day 1

Hi!

Welcome to the first day of your wondrous journey toward health and vitality. I'm looking forward to our time together! As I'm writing this, it's 4 A.M. I have a tradition of waking up very early because it's the quietest time of the day. I love to listen to the silence.

In the stillness of this cold, starlit morning, I'm deeply inspired by the path that lies before us. I know that during our time together, something precious and powerful will emerge. I'm not sure exactly what form it will take for you, but it feels mighty and awesome—a great and grand adventure toward radiant well-being.

Your future is created by the choices you make and—as surely as the sun rises—if you make the decision today to change your life and empower your body, the forces of the universe will unite to propel you in that direction. As you embark on this program, remember this: The quality of your health determines the quality of your life. The better you feel, the easier it is to manifest your dreams (and support the dreams of others). The journey to strengthen and heal your body is a sacred one.

On this program, when you finally gather the determination to transform your physical self, the aftermath isn't always easy. Sometimes people around you become threatened by the changes they see in you because it might make them feel inadequate. There may even be times when you doubt your own progress. That's all right. Allow yourself to experience those feelings, then continue on. Today's exercises are some of the most time-consuming for the month, so hang in there. Do the best you can, and enjoy the process.

May the coming 28 days allow more light and radiance to shine through every cell in your body, illuminating every aspect of your life.

With all my love,
Denise

Day 1 (Air): Health and Body Assessment

The journey to vibrant health begins with stark honesty about where you are. Be forthright in your self-appraisal.

Affirmation for the Day

My evaluation of my body is not who I am.

Today

Periodically take enormous deep breaths, imagining the life-force energy filling your lungs and every cell in your body.

Reward

My reward for completing Day 1 is:

(Gift yourself this reward at the successful completion of today's exercises.)

Overview

- *Committed to Change!*
  Level 1: Where? What? Why?

- *Going for It!*
  Level 2: Assessing Your Health and Your Body: Where Are You Now?

- *Playing Full Out!*
  Level 3: Regarding Your Body: What's the Truth?

Level 1: Where? What? Why?

Spend some time thinking about the following questions, and write down your responses in your Process Journal.

—— *Where are you now?* Take a couple of minutes to think about where you are regarding your health. Jot down a quick assessment.

—— *What do you want?* Write out your intention for the next 28 days. In other words, what are the *exact* results you desire for your body and your health after completing this program? Be specific. *Where intention goes, energy flows.* What are your goals for doing this program? Additionally, what could you achieve or experience in life—that you currently aren't—if your health were truly radiant?

— *Why must you absolutely do something <u>now</u> to boost your health?* What are the potential *consequences* in the future if you don't take action today? It's essential that you answer this question. Seriously, what will the cost be if you don't start to make some changes to improve your health? Will your self-esteem suffer? Might your relationships be impacted? Will you potentially suffer pain and/or discomfort? Will your life expectancy be shortened? Will you have less energy? How might it affect your ability to get health insurance (or the cost to maintain it)? Will it dampen your opportunities to spend time with loved ones or to travel? Could it increase your chances of having a heart attack, diabetes, joint damage, or other illnesses or diseases? What are the potential long-term health consequences if you don't make some changes? If walking 30 minutes a day could reduce your chances of having a heart attack, diabetes, or painful joints, would you be willing to do it? If not, why? If yes, what's stopping you?

Level 2: Assessing Your Health and Your Body: Where Are You Now?

It's difficult to get where you want to go if you don't know where you are. On any journey, when you look at the map, you need to know your destination. You also need to know your starting point so that you can get to your objective. If you don't know where you are (or where you're going), you may get lost as you venture out. This exercise will help you discover where your starting point is regarding your health.

Today, start to assess where you are physically. You can sketch a simple outline of your body and draw arrows to different places with notations about the general health of each area (such as glands, organs, skin, bones, muscle tone, and so on). Alternatively, you could list different parts of your body in your Process Journal with an assessment next to it. Whichever method you choose, review every aspect of your body and be as detailed as possible.

For example, you might write something like this in your journal:

- *Feet:* The joint in my right toe aches.

- *Toes:* The little toe on my left foot is growing at a strange angle, and it hurts sometimes.

Take time to become clear on your current state of health and what your goals are. If you want to get your blood pressure down, for instance, note what it is right now so you have a starting point and where you'd like it to be in the future. Perhaps you can presently walk up one flight of stairs without getting winded, and your goal is to easily climb three flights of stairs. Write this down. Or maybe when you bend over you can only touch your knees with the tips of your fingers, and your goal is to touch the floor with ease. Write this down, too! If your goal is to have more muscle definition and/or drop weight and inches, then make sure that you know your current measurements. Keep all of this information in your Process Journal.

Whenever you're working toward improving your health, it's good to have a baseline. A physical exam and blood tests can give you an objective assessment of your current state and may help you clarify your specific health goals. (If you're overdue for a physical, you might consider scheduling one now.)

Level 3: Regarding Your Body: What's the Truth?

In order to gain an incredible amount of value out of this program, it's essential that you take time to tell yourself the truth about your body and health. This Level 3 exercise is a way to achieve this. (It potentially takes more time than any other exercise in this program, but it's worth it.)

What Is the Truth about Your Health Priorities?

Your health is a reflection of your lifestyle. To obtain a clear picture of which actions and behaviors support your health (and which don't), do this important exercise. Create a pie chart on a poster board that illustrates how you spend your time (waking hours). Give a percentage to each activity in your normal day. This is your *actual* "Life-as-Pie" chart. Then make a second one that shows how you'd like to spend your hours. This is your *desired* Life-as-Pie chart.

Start off by making a list of your personal categories for pie slices. Create your categories according to your own life. Here's an example of a woman who completed the exercise; note her self-described categories and the percentages she assigned for each of them. These are the slices of her actual Life-as-Pie chart:

- **Work:** 60 percent *(computer time, work-related travel, e-mail, meetings, overtime)*

- **Recreation:** 10 percent *(television, books, DVDs, concerts)*

- **Personal Hygiene:** 5 percent *(showers, baths, makeup, hair, nails)*

- **Meals:** 4 percent *(preparing and eating meals, drinking tea, food shopping)*

- **Friends:** 4 percent *(conversations on the phone, e-mails, restaurants)*

- **Acquaintances:** 4 percent *(events, parties)*

- **Shopping:** 3 percent *(clothes, house, personal)*

- **Family:** 2 percent *(conversations, phone calls)*

- **Cleaning:** 2 percent *(daily room by room)*

- **Clutter-Clearing/Home Repair:** 2 percent *(home, garage, yard)*

- **Health:** 1 percent *(walking, taking vitamins)*

- **Relaxing:** 1 percent *(napping, watching birds, petting cats)*

- **Creativity:** 1 percent *(painting, arranging flowers, gardening)*

- **Spirit:** 1 percent *(meditating, being still in nature)*

Once you create your own chart, stand back to see how much of it actually contributes to your health and vitality, how much detracts from it, and how much is neutral. If only a small percentage of your day enhances your vitality, draw up a new pie chart of how you *could* spend your time to empower your health. Be truthful! Choose things that you love to do, you might do, or you could learn to love to do on a regular basis. (This is for you only; you aren't being judged or graded on your pie chart.) For instance, if you have chronic back pain, you might not want to join your local hula-hoop club . . . yet. But you could carve out time to do some stretching.

As you look at your *desired* Life-as-Pie chart, ask yourself these questions:

1. *Is this accurate? Is this <u>really</u> how I want to spend my time?*

2. *What needs to happen for my ideal to become my reality?*

3. *If this is truly how I want to spend my time, then what do I need to change in order for this to happen?*

4. *Will I do it? Why? When? How?*

As a suggestion, color and decorate your desired pie chart so that it brings you joy every time you look at it. The more attention you put toward it, the more it will begin to feel like an emerging reality. In addition, write down the answers to the following questions in your Process Journal.

1. How do I *really* feel about my body?

2. Is there anything that I resent, hate, or dislike about my body?

3. Is there anything that I absolutely love and admire about my body?

4. What is great about my particular body?

5. What have I been putting off regarding my body?

6. What does my body say about me to the world?

7. If my body were a metaphor for my life, what would the message be?

8. How do others see my body?

9. What judgments do I think my family or friends make about my body?

10. Does my body express who I feel I am to others?

11. Is there anything I need to forgive (including myself or others) in regard to my body?

12. What are my most important goals concerning my body? What has kept me from meeting them in the past?

13. Will I allow these blockages to keep me from achieving my health goals in the future?

14. What will the quality of my life be like if I don't attain my health goals?

15. Am I truly committed to achieving my goals? Why or why not?

People who fail to make positive life changes usually get stopped by frustration, which is then followed by procrastination. When you feel frustrated, take a moment and use the time as an opportunity to strengthen your resolve. Breathe deeply and plunge ahead. This is usually when the greatest breakthroughs occur!

⚛ ⚛ ⚛

You made it through Day 1, which is a huge feat. Way to go! Don't forget to claim your reward—you deserve it! Although you spent the day evaluating your body, please know that *your assessment is not who you are.* Remember to acknowledge and celebrate all of your accomplishments. You've begun a glorious adventure to unlock your inner wisdom and activate your vitality. Congratulations!

D a y   2

Hi!

The wind is howling today. Even though it's an Air Day, I didn't expect this much air! I thought the roof was going to blow off the barn today because it was shaking so much.

You've made it to Day 2. Congratulations! There's power in momentum, and the first couple of days are important to build the foundation and impetus for what's ahead. (Day 1 takes a substantial amount of time—it gets easier after this.) Even though you're just beginning, beneath the surface things are already starting to change.

I'm assuming that on your first day:

1. *You took time to take an honest look at where you are physically.*

2. *You're clear on what your intention is for this program.*

3. *You're now ready to continue your 28-day program.*

Did you give yourself a gift for successfully completing the first day? If you feel like you blew it on Day 1, today is a new day. Look forward—don't look back. Remember that things are already happening . . . in spite of your judgments about how well you've done so far.

Today's focus is on commitment. Oftentimes, this word is associated with another person; however, the most important commitment you can make is to yourself. When you're committed to your soul's journey, you learn how to say no to others in loving ways so that you can say yes to your own well-being. The commitments you make today are significant and will magnify your results from this program.

Here's to a stunning Day 2!

All my love,

Denise

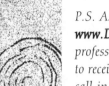

P.S. As a suggestion, you might consider going to **www.DeniseLinn.com** or **www.Soul-Coaching.com** to find a professional certified Soul Coach to work with you. If you'd like to receive live coaching from me directly, check out my weekly call-in radio show, *Soul Coaching,* on **HayHouseRadio.com**.

Day 2 (Air): Making a Commitment to Your Body

Now that you've assessed your current health—and you're also beginning to get clear on where you'd like to be in the future—the next step is to make a commitment to take action. *This is an act of power.* The instant that you truly decide to change your life through empowering your body, you put forces in play that almost magically begin to transform your health, vigor, and energy fields.

<u>Affirmation for the Day</u>

I am committed to empowering my body.

Today

Breathe deeply and fully. Hold for a few seconds, then exhale completely. This kind of breath is considered holy, for it's rejuvenating and renewing. As you inhale, imagine that you're filling your entire being with the living energy of the cosmos. And as you exhale, visualize releasing all that is not needed in your life. Repeat this breath throughout the day.

Reward

My reward for completing Day 2 is:

(Gift yourself this reward at the successful completion of today's exercises.)

Overview

- *Committed to Change!*
  Level 1: Commit to Taking One Empowering Action Daily

- *Going for It!*
  Level 2: What Are Your Values Regarding Your Body?

- *Playing Full Out!*
  Level 3: Concerning Your Health: What Have You Been Putting Off? (And the Miracle Box!)

Level 1: Commit to Taking One Empowering Action Daily

1. Could Do

Make a detailed list of *all* of the things that you *could* do to revitalize your body, such as taking vitamins (list them), doing yoga or tai chi, stretching, walking, hiking, running, reciting affirmations, avoiding refined sugar and alcohol, meditating, practicing breathing exercises, wearing magnetic bracelets, eating raw foods, alternating hot and cold showers, getting massages or acupuncture, and so on.

2. Might Do

Now circle the things on the list that you *might* actually do consistently during the remaining 27 days.

3. Will Do

Review what you've circled, and check off the items that you absolutely know for sure you *will* do for the next four weeks. What are you totally committed to doing to empower your health? Don't worry if your list is now very short. Even if you checked off just one thing you know for sure that you'll do, this is good.

Ask yourself if you're *really* going to keep your commitment . . . and if not, what commitment could you keep? Tell the truth. You know yourself—you know what you will and won't do. Choose at least one thing, and make a covenant with yourself to keep your word regarding that item. Your word is law in *your* universe. Make a vow to yourself with the integrity and intensity that you'd have if you were giving your word to the Creator.

Here are some examples of daily commitments for your health:

- Meditate for five minutes.
- Stretch for ten minutes.
- Sit still for ten minutes.
- Take a nightly candlelit bath.
- Drink six glasses of water each day.
- Write down exactly what foods you eat every day.
- Walk for ten minutes.
- Clutter-clear for ten minutes.
- Spend five minutes in nature.
- Eat breakfast every morning.

Level 2: What Are Your Values Regarding Your Body?

Your values create your identity, and they have a *profound* effect on your health. In fact, they manifest in the way in which your body looks, feels, and moves. In truth, your entire life revolves around them, so it's essential to discover what they are. (These *values* aren't morals; they represent what you truly cherish in life, to the exclusion of other things.)

Watch people walking through a mall; you can tell so much about what they value just by the way they express themselves through their bodies. You can often tell if a person is depressed, confident, shy, or sad. To experience peak health, it's vital to discover what you hold sacred . . . and then live your life in alignment with it. There are no "right" values—just the ones that are right for *you.*

Here are several examples:

Abundance	Flexibility	Peace
Acceptance	Freedom	Perfection
Adventure	Friendship	Productivity
Comfort	Growth	Safety
Courage	Integrity	Security
Creativity	Intelligence	Spirituality
Determination	Joy	Vitality
Endurance	Knowledge	
Family	Love	

In your Process Journal, write down all your values. Then decide which ones are most important and which are least important. When you're finished, look at your top value and ask yourself: *What kind of movement might be consistent with this value?* In other words, a body that typifies "freedom" might move in an expansive manner, with a spine and limbs that are flexible and fluid. A body that exemplifies "peace" might move slowly and elegantly and take relaxed, deep breaths. Is your body expression consistent with your top values? Write down all of your thoughts in your Process Journal.

As you examine your values, ask yourself—regarding your health—if your life is aligned with your values. For example, if one of your top values is "adventure," but you're too out of shape to go on an excursion or outing, then you may need to consider reevaluating what you hold sacred (or transforming your body to match what you value).

On the other hand, if your top value is "comfort" yet you're consistently challenging your body to climb mountains and barrel down black-diamond slopes, then you may need to change your values (or else transform the way you use your body) so that your body and your values are consistent. *If your body is not congruent with your values, a deep disharmony will exist within you and your health will suffer.*

Level 3: Concerning Your Health:
What Have You Been Putting Off? (And the Miracle Box!)

Regarding your health, *what have you been putting off?* Have you been meaning to schedule a physical, visit your dentist, have a mole removed, or pull your exercise bike out of the garage? Make a list of what you've been putting off, and then *take action today* on at least one item. (In addition, make a plan to take every one of those items to completion in the future. Put it in writing, and post it where you can easily see it. Cross off items as they're completed.) When you make a commitment and keep your word, you're on the road to true inner mastery.

Creating a Miracle Box for Health

This is magic! I'm not quite sure exactly how it works, but it does. Hundreds of people have shared their miracles with me as a result of making and using their Miracle Box. Here's what you need to do:

Get a box: pick out an old shoe box, make your own, or buy one. Decorate it and designate this as your mystical container. This is no longer an ordinary box—so make it as beautiful as you can, inside and out.

Your Miracle Box is a way to:

1. Gain clarity regarding your health

2. Declare your intentions to the universe regarding your body

3. Ask for spiritual assistance to attain your
   health goals

It works like this: On small pieces of paper, write down your sincere desires regarding your body. You can address them to the Universal Manager, Creator, or your Higher Self. Be specific and use the present tense, *as if it has already been delivered to you!* Write one statement per piece of paper. For example, if you're working on improving your eyesight, you might write: *My eyesight is excellent, and I see beauty all around me.* If you wish to diminish chronic back problems, jot down something like: *I walk easily, joyously, and effortlessly.*

Make the pieces of paper beautiful, too. On one piece, you might wish: *I know that miracles are happening for my body, all in accordance with my highest good!*

Be creative! You could even spray your Miracle Box with your favorite essential oils to make it smell as good as it looks, or place beautiful stones or flower petals in it. On the inside lid, write: *All that is in this box is True!* Also, wherever you want, write: *Thank you! Thank You! Thank You!* Then put your box in a special place with the intent that all prayers within it are answered in alignment with your highest good. Whenever you have a new request, write it out and place it in the box. And when one of your desires is granted or fulfilled, remove the slip of paper . . . and offer your sincere gratitude!

⚜ ⚜ ⚜

Day 3

Hi!

You've made it for two days. Small changes are already taking place . . . even if you're not consciously aware of them. It's happening!

But what if you feel like you've blown it already? What if you haven't kept your commitments, and it's only the beginning of Day 3? As a suggestion, think about what you'd tell a friend if she were doing this program and had sheepishly admitted to you that she slipped up. Would you say, "What a slouch! You'll never get any results!" I kind of doubt it.

I think you'd respond with something like this: "Don't focus on what you didn't do—celebrate what you did accomplish! And then recommit to the program!" Or maybe you'd say, "Perhaps your commitments are too hard to attain. Consider revisiting them, and stick with only the ones that you know you can keep." Please remember to treat yourself with as much kindness as you would a dear friend.

As I've said earlier, this program works even if you don't do it perfectly. Once you've signed up, you entered through a sacred gateway that's allowing energies of the universe to work with you and through you, in ways you can't fully comprehend. It is happening! Trust and believe!

You have my love!

Denise

P.S. Did you remember to gift yourself your reward for yesterday? I hope so. You don't need to suffer to grow. Your journey to health should be enjoyable!

Day 3 (Air): Create the Space for Health Miracles: Free Yourself from Clutter

Do you have too much stuff? Does it drag you down? This could be contributing to tiredness, being overweight, or numerous other health problems. Today is the beginning of clutter-clearing, which can make an enormous difference in your physical well-being.

Of course, it might seem totally illogical that clutter in the home can impact (or reflect) your health. However, the ancient art of feng shui—which includes understanding the negative impact of clutter—has survived for centuries for the simple reason that it works. The energy and objects in your home significantly affect your body. In my many years as a feng-shui practitioner and teacher, I found overwhelming proof of this strong correlation. For example, if clients had a lot of clutter in their hallways that made it difficult to maneuver throughout the house, it wasn't unusual for those individuals to also experience difficulties with their circulation system. When clients had cluttered spiral staircases in the center of the home, it wasn't out of the ordinary for them to have heart challenges. If the areas around air ducts for the heating or cooling system were cluttered or clogged, my clients occasionally exhibited lung problems. People who suffer ill effects from being overweight often have lots of unneeded stuff clogging their homes. It's as if their home is also overweight.

If one of the reasons you're doing this program is to lose some weight, then clutter-clearing is very important. To help dissolve excess pounds (your internal clutter) from your body, remove the things you don't need from your house. You'll begin to notice a difference in the way you feel immediately!

Is there a particular area of your body that needs healing or strengthening? Notice if there's a place in your home that might represent that area, and clutter-clear that space. If you're having problems with your eyes, for instance, maybe it's time to clean or repair the windows. If you have lots of knickknacks crowded on your windowsills, you might want to cull the herd. (In feng shui, windows represent your eyes.) As you do so, affirm: *As I clear my windows, I am gaining greater clarity of vision!*

Clutter is anything that you don't use or don't love. To step into more vitality and balance in your body, clear out the clutter in your home. With every item, ask yourself: *Do I love this? Do I use this? Have I used this in the last two years?* Even if you don't believe in feng shui, try clearing some of your clutter and see if you don't notice a change in the way you feel. It can work like magic!

Affirmation for the Day
There is clarity within my body and around me.

Today

Breathe in acceptance and appreciation for your body, and breathe out any judgments you may be harboring.

Reward

My reward for completing Day 3 is:

(Gift yourself this reward at the successful completion of today's exercises.)

Overview

- *Committed to Change!*
  Level 1: Clutter-Clear One Area

- *Going for It!*
  Level 2: Clutter-Clear a Larger Area

- *Playing Full Out!*
  Level 3: Completely Clutter-Clear One Room

Level 1: Clutter-Clear One Area

Clutter-clearing can be a powerful and transformational process. Choose one small area in your home that symbolizes health to you and clutter-clear it. In feng shui, the rooms usually associated with this are the kitchen, bathroom, bedroom, and also the center of the house. If you don't know where to start, consider picking one of these areas. For example, if there's a drawer in your bathroom where you keep vitamins or medications, start there. Take everything out of the drawer, and wash or wipe it down. Hold this thought as you do so: *My body is becoming healthier and clearer.* Only put the items that you actually use back into the drawer. If any are expired, toss them. As you reorganize, do so with the intention that you're bringing shining energy into your body. (If time is an issue, then only clear one small part of the drawer.)

Level 2: Clutter-Clear a Larger Area

Choose a larger area that symbolizes health to you. Words have power, so when you say affirmations at the same time as you clear an area of your home, this speaks directly to the subconscious mind. Create an affirmation that matches what you're doing. For example, if you're clearing out your refrigerator, you might affirm: *All of the food that I eat energizes and heals my body.*

If you're working in your bathroom, although the items on the countertops might be necessary, perhaps they could be presented in a more attractive way. Is it really necessary to have all of the lotions, razors, toothbrushes, makeup, prescriptions, supplements, mouthwashes, and hair dryer spread out in full view? Is there a more harmonious way to arrange them? Maybe some of these items could be placed in a beautiful basket.

Level 3: Completely Clutter-Clear One Room

Clutter-clearing shouldn't be an arduous duty; it should be a exhilarating event! If you have piles of stuff weighing you down, sapping your energy, and creating stagnation in your life, it's time for a clean sweep. As you clutter-clear an entire room, ask yourself: *Do I use this? Do I love this? Have I used this in the last two years?* Then as you free yourself from clutter, affirm: *The more I clear, the more vibrant and alive my body becomes!*

If you're not sure which room to start in, begin in the bedroom, bedroom closet, or bathroom. These are all places where you refresh, revitalize, and nurture yourself. When you're finished, light a candle and sit down. Quietly say a blessing for your health. You may also wish to put out fresh flowers or display some artwork that makes you feel vibrant and healthy just looking at it.

🕸 🕸 🕸

Day 4

Hi!

Whew, the wind is blowing like crazy today. The weather station says that it's 40 miles per hour with gusts much higher. It feels dramatic and exhilarating. It really makes it feel like I'm in Air Week!

Well, you've made it to Day 4. Have you been rewarding yourself for the exercises that you've completed? It's important to celebrate your successes; it's positive reinforcement. It might seem silly to you, but after a while there's a subconscious part of you that will look forward to the reward—hence, the program becomes easier to follow.

Have you been keeping your commitment to do something every day to empower your health? Even if it's a tiny action, it's a step toward your goals. If not, recommit yourself. Keep going!

Last night as I was lying in bed listening to the wind, I affirmed: "I love you. I love you. I love you," over and over to my body. I think that my body loved to hear that because it feels so good today. Sometimes I think our bodies are a bit like children: if a child is told that she's wonderful, strong, or beautiful, she responds accordingly; and if she's told that she's worthless or undesirable, she also reacts accordingly. In the past, I haven't always been very kind in the ways in which I communicated with my physical self, but right now I really do love my body. It continues to work brilliantly in spite of the damage it has received.

Don't be concerned if you suddenly become more aware of aches and pains in your body. Chances are that these sensations aren't new; you're just now consciously experiencing them instead of suppressing them. For example, maybe you've had neck pain for so long that you don't even notice it anymore. During this program, you may become more aware of that discomfort in your neck. But this is a good thing. The more aware you are of your body, the easier it is to heal and strengthen it.

All my love,
Denise

Day 4 (Air): What Are Your Inner Beliefs about Your Body?

You have beliefs about your body. (We all do.) Many of these inner beliefs are empowering, yet some have a damaging effect on you and there is value in examining them.

Beliefs are just thoughts that have been held for a long time—you didn't consciously choose most of them. You were programmed—for many years—by the belief systems of your parents, other family members, your culture, and the environment you grew up in. (And keep in mind that your parents and others were programmed by *their* parents, family, and so on.) When you were a child, for example, maybe everyone told you that you were similar to Aunt Polly, who had bad eyesight. After some time, you may begin to assume that you'd have bad eyesight just like Aunt Polly. Your body responds powerfully to the thoughts that you carry. If you fully expected to have eye problems, it's much more likely that you would eventually develop them instead of someone who doesn't carry that specific belief.

Someone else has probably shaped your beliefs about your body and how you perceive it. However, part of your inner power is the ability to *shape your own perceptions* of yourself—and thus be able to direct your own physical destiny. Through this, you can begin to create the body that you desire.

The first step is to discover what some of your beliefs about your body are. The next step is to begin to relinquish any that don't serve you . . . and to embrace those that do.

Affirmation for the Day

I love and accept my body.
It is splendid just as it is.

Today

Observe your body with the mind-set that it's neither good nor bad—it's just the body that you occupy. Also pay attention to the thoughts you have about your body, and acknowledge that they're neither good nor bad. They're just the thoughts you have about your body.

Reward

My reward for completing Day 4 is:

(Gift yourself this reward at the successful completion of today's exercises.)

<u>Overview</u>

- *Committed to Change!*
  Level 1: What Do You Believe about Your Body?

- *Going for It!*
  Level 2: Your So-Called Physical Faults Can Be Virtues

- *Playing Full Out!*
  Level 3: Observing Your Core Beliefs about Your Body

Level 1: What Do You Believe about Your Body?

What do you believe about your body? This isn't what you *should* believe or what you'd *like* to think is true. The question is what do you *really* believe about your body and your health? Don't judge the thoughts that come to mind—just observe them.

Write the following statement in your Process Journal, and then complete it, jotting down all thoughts that arise. Below it are some examples:

"I believe that my body . . ."

. . . is ugly
. . . will never get in shape
. . . might get breast cancer (my mother had it)
. . . has a slow metabolism
. . . has brittle bones

. . . is my saboteur

. . . has good endurance

. . . is stuck with cellulite forever

. . . can't tolerate wheat

. . . shouldn't have coffee

. . . will never drop its extra weight

. . . can heal faster with chicken soup

. . . is weak

. . . heals slowly

. . . is in great shape

. . . can easily become fit and toned

. . . is healthy and strong

. . . has a great metabolism

. . . has strong bones

. . . is my saving grace

. . . is easily sculpted and transformed

. . . is able to digest almost everything

. . . thrives with coffee

. . . can easily drop extra weight

After each item on your list, relax, look within, and ask yourself this question: *Is this really true?* For example, if you wrote "I believe that my body is ugly," ask yourself if this is indeed a factual statement. (In other words, you might *believe* that your body is ugly, but is this *really* true?) Then write the answer that comes up for you, perhaps something like: "Actually, that's not a true statement. The truth is that there are some aspects of my body that are very attractive."

When you're finished, ask yourself this question after each statement: *For me to feel this way about my body, what would I have to believe about myself and the world?* Write down your responses. Here are a few samples: "To believe that my body is ugly, I would need to believe that the airbrushed images of bodies in magazines are an accurate portrayal of beauty," or "To believe that my body is ugly, I would need to believe that there is only one standard of beauty."

You can choose your beliefs! *You* are the one who determines which beliefs you keep and which ones you discard. And remember that *nothing has meaning until you give it meaning.* So why not decide to hold empowering beliefs about your body?

Level 2: Your So-Called Physical Faults Can Be Virtues

When you unconditionally accept your body, it works better and your energy level rises. To move toward acceptance, sometimes you have to think outside the box to discover what's great about the things that you normally judge. This might seem silly, but it can help you love "what is." For example, if you believe that you're carrying too much weight on your thighs, start to think about all the things that are great about that (even if it seems absurd to you) such as: you're going to have a much softer ride on a bicycle; if there's a famine, you're going to live longer than the skinny people with no extra weight; or if Rubenesque bodies come back into fashion, you're going to be ready! I know this may seem ridiculous, but anything that you can do to totally love and appreciate your body and see it in a positive light will be an empowering, activating force for your health.

Additionally, it's a law of the universe that what you resist persists; therefore, the more time and energy you spend resisting those hips, the more you "create" those thunder thighs. Love them, cherish them, and even be thrilled to have them . . . and it's so much easier to create what you desire. If you spend valuable time and energy hating something, you are actually helping it manifest. *What you resist persists!*

Make a list of your body's so-called faults in your Process Journal. Then next to each "fault," write ways in which it can be viewed in a positive manner or what benefits or "virtues" it gives you.

Level 3: Observing Your Core Beliefs about Your Body

A core belief is a notion you've held for so long that it has become entrenched in your subconscious mind, dictating your health and the way your body feels. These beliefs are like a hum in the background that you don't realize is there until it stops. List positive and negative core beliefs that you have about your body in your Process Journal.

After writing your list, think back to when you first adopted each belief and note that. Perhaps one of your core beliefs is that you'll have heart problems as you get older. As you explore your memory to discover when you first adopted this belief, you remember your grand-mother telling you, when you were seven years old, that all the men in your family died from heart failure at a young age. Although you consciously forgot the conversation, the statement was imbedded in your mind from that point forward.

Here are more examples of negative core beliefs about your health:

- "No pain, no gain! When I exercise, it has to hurt to do any good."

- "Everyone in my family is overweight, so of course, I will be, too."

- "I never have any time to take care of my body."

- "I always get sick every winter."

- "If you don't start working on your health when you're young, you can never be in top shape later in life."

The following are examples of *positive* core beliefs:

- "My body has an incredible immune system."

- "The more I love my body, the healthier I am."

- "My body is attracted to the exact foods that it needs."

- "I have really good teeth."
- "I'm going to live to a very old age."

By simply discovering the root of a belief, you can begin to release it from your energy fields. (You *do* have the ability to release negative core beliefs and create positive ones instead.)

☘ ☘ ☘

Day 5

Hi!

Although I believe in synchronicity—and I know that it's Air Week—the wild wind that continues to blow here at Summerhill Ranch is ridiculous. It has already blown apart one of our gazebos, which is now just a twisted heap of metal. Dead branches are being ripped off the old oak trees, too. It was as if the wind was clutter-clearing the trees!

One of today's exercises is about clearing clutter around your front door. (In feng shui, if one wants to be incredibly healthy, it's important that this particular area is clear.) For the last few years, I've had two old orchid plants that were right inside the front door. Even though they didn't look very good, I kept them because I felt sorry for them. But then I finally reminded myself that there's no death, only change, and that it was time to replace those plants with healthy, vital ones. (Good-bye, little buddies. Have a good time recycling back to Mother Earth!)

The fact that you've made it to Day 5 is excellent! This is often a turning point. If you can make it to Day 5, you can make it through the entire program. Have you been fulfilling your daily commitment? If not, you might want to think about choosing something that you can keep. It's all right to do this. It's okay to shift gears midstream. Make commitments you can keep. Also, don't forget to <u>breathe</u> deeply and fully over and over again. During Air Week, it's crucial to use your breath to oxygenate the cells in your body.

All my love,
Denise

Day 5 (Air): Energy Up—Energy Down

Whenever you feel joy, you literally begin to shine. This radiant glow is made up of zillions of tiny sparkles, which generate an energy field that flows outward from your body into the world around you. The sparkles also magnetize energy to flow into you. Because of these radiant currents, your life force expands. Your entire body is strengthened, and as a result, your life is filled with clarity and vitality.

The Spirit of Air relates to the mental aspect of self and also to your ability to have clarity about your life and body. Just as you take a breath to help you focus and think clearly when you need to make an important decision, your breath—and the Spirit of Air—is always nudging you in the right direction. For today's exercises, you'll begin to see what expands your energy (and what diminishes it), and you'll also choose areas to clutter-clear that relate to your health.

Affirmation for the Day
Radiant, sparkling energy fills my body!

Today
Breathe deeply and fully. When you breathe with consciousness and awareness, this is holy. Ancient mystics understood this, which is why they put so much emphasis on breath.

Reward
My reward for completing Day 5 is:

(Gift yourself this reward at the successful
completion of today's exercises.)

Overview

- *Committed to Change!*
  Level 1: Energy Up—Energy Down

- *Going for It!*
  Level 2: Clutter-Clearing for Your Health

- *Playing Full Out!*
  Level 3: Metaphors for Health

Level 1: Energy Up—Energy Down

Every single experience you have will either take your body's energy up or down (or it will be neutral). The practice called *muscle testing* chronicles this effect on our bodies. For example, if you think about pleasant memories, your muscle strength increases, but if you switch to something that depresses you, your muscle strength decreases. You're normally not consciously aware of these subtle changes—nevertheless, your body is *always* responding to everything and everyone around you.

The secret is to know when your energy is shifting. As a suggestion, visualize a meter that has negative numbers on the left and positive numbers on the right (or picture negative numbers below a line and positives above it). The arm of the meter is at zero, which is neutral. This device monitors your level, letting you know if you're losing or gaining energy. Periodically today, close your eyes and imagine that you can see where the arm of your meter is sitting.

A good way to test your internal meter is to drink some water. Almost always, the meter you're visualizing will go up when you hydrate your body. You can try different foods and then notice which ones take your meter up and which drive it down. Also be aware of people, places, and things that affect your level. Awareness is power. Throughout the day, notice what's increasing your sparkle and what's decreasing it.

Level 2: Clutter-Clearing for Your Health

Clutter equals stagnant energy. In order for your energy to flow, clutter *must* be cleared. Your home should be a relaxing retreat that supports your body's rejuvenation. However, if it's piled up with too much "stuff," it can make you feel mentally overwhelmed with all the things that you've been putting off but need to finish. This can lead to stress-related illnesses, chronic diseases, or exhaustion. The unfortunate thing about clutter is that all too often, it spirals out of control, which makes it easy to become overly anxious and stressed.

You've already started your clutter-clearing this week. Today is the time to continue. (Remember: *love it, use it, or release it.*) Choose one room in your home and for every object that you see, ask yourself: *Does this empower me? Does it diminish me?* Surround yourself with objects that make you *feel* vibrant and alive. Release objects that make you feel tired, lethargic, or depressed.

Pay particular attention to the center of your home. This is an area that in feng shui relates to your overall health. It should be clutter free and clean (especially if it's a bathroom or if it's unusually dark). Another significant place is your front door, which *sets* the energy of your entire house and should be clear of clutter. Check that your door opens freely and without any creaking sounds. Make sure that the very first thing you see when you enter your home is something that gives a feeling of health and vitality.

Level 3: Metaphors for Health

The objects in your home are invested with symbolism and meaning; therefore, clearing things out can have a direct effect on your psyche and ultimately your health. I've heard of a program in Scandinavia in which volunteers would go into the homes of cancer patients to help them sort through and clear out things before they died. However, it was soon discovered that the patients' condition often dramatically improved in direct correlation with removing unneeded items from their homes. This gives credence to the idea that when you clear your clutter, you improve your health.

Start small. Choose one area that could symbolically be related to your health issues. As you clutter-clear, ask yourself, *If this represented something about my health, what would it be?* Then as you tackle that area, recite affirmations to validate the health of that part of your body. For example, as you clutter-clear objects off the floor, you might affirm: *My health foundations are strong and vibrant.* You can choose the meanings for the metaphors you create.

Here are some more suggestions: If you have lung issues, make sure that all of your things aren't shoved together because too much stuff "suffocates." Clutter around the toilet should be removed if you have elimination problems. Do you have challenges with your mouth or teeth? If so, clear around the front door. If you want to drop extra weight, look for hidden clutter that's shoved into closets, storage units, or drawers. Keeping an item because you might need it someday is like your body holding on to excess fat because someday you might need it to survive a famine. Storing clutter for some potential future use—even though you haven't needed it for ten years—is a negative affirmation. It tells your subconscious mind: *I never use this, and I'm okay without it now. However, I might not be okay in the future, so I better keep it.*

If you have lots of things that you're keeping for this reason, this can be a self-fulfilling prophecy of a future filled with a lack of the things you need. Get rid of this clutter because doing so sends a powerful message to your subconscious mind that you *will* be fine in the future. It tells your body: *You don't need to hold on to that weight to see me through a potential lean time in the future.*

Many people report profound changes in their bodies —including dropping weight—simply from clearing out old, unused clutter. Write down what you cleared in your Process Journal.

✿ ✿ ✿

Day 6

Hi!

The winds last night were from 50 to 75 mph! This is hurricane strength. The UPS driver told us yesterday that he had to stop making deliveries because he couldn't stand up without being blown over. Air Week—whew!

You can't hear the secret messages from your body if your life is clogged with clutter, so I'm clutter-clearing at the same time as you are. I went through everything in the refrigerator and got rid of items that I hadn't used in months—condiments with Asian names that I couldn't pronounce, fish oil, a pickle jar with one lone shriveled pickle, and so forth. To me a toned body means a "toned refrigerator," and since I don't want any more excess on my body, this (to me) means that there shouldn't be any excess in my refrigerator.

I also experienced a humongous bummer yesterday. When I was clutter-clearing, I found my Intention List for my body from 25 years ago, and although I'd manifested so much on my list, I got discouraged because there were many things that I've desired for more than two decades yet still hadn't attained them. To climb out of this self-imposed hole, I thought about what advice I'd give a friend in the same situation, and here's what I'd say:

- You are enough, just as you are.

- Even if you failed in the past, this doesn't mean that you'll fail in the future. The past does not need to equal the future.

- It's never too late to change, and change doesn't need to be big. It starts with small steps.

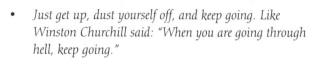

- *Just get up, dust yourself off, and keep going. Like Winston Churchill said: "When you are going through hell, keep going."*

- *Cherish and celebrate what's working, and fill your heart with gratitude for the incredible, immense blessings in your life.*

I decided to take my own advice, so I dusted myself off and accepted that I may never reach all my goals. (Well, I don't completely accept this, but that's okay, too.)
With immense love,
Denise

Day 6 (Air): Lightening Up—Letting Go While Doing More Clutter-Clearing

On a subconscious level, many people define themselves through and by their "stuff." It's what I call the I-am-what-I-own syndrome. They don't own their stuff— their stuff owns *them,* and it can have a deep impact on their physical health. Moreover, clutter can come in many forms. Of course, there's the typical home clutter, but there are also other kinds, including outdated files on your computer that you'll never use, old receipts, or a garden that's choked with overgrown plants and weeds.

Your clutter can even be internal. If you work too much and don't see your friends or family, your time is cluttered. If you continually talk without listening or you're always worrying, analyzing, or thinking in a frenetic way, then your mind is cluttered. And if you're constantly angry, fearful, or resentful of people or situations in your life, then your heart is cluttered . . . and every kind of clutter affects your body and your health. Today, you'll be doing internal clutter-clearing.

Affirmation for the Day
No matter what is occurring
in my body, I am safe.

Today
Relax. Listen to soothing music; or read inspiring books, poems, or passages. Put your feet up and stretch out. Breathe. Be.

Reward
My reward for completing Day 6 is:

(Gift yourself this reward at the successful completion of today's exercises.)

Overview

- *Committed to Change!*
  Level 1: Zen Moment

- *Going for It!*
  Level 2: Clutter-Clearing Your Identity

- *Playing Full Out!*
  Level 3: Clear Mental Clutter

Level 1: Zen Moment

We often aren't present in our bodies. We're either thinking about the future or dwelling in the past, yet our bodies are *always* trying to tell us something, and it's important to take a moment to discover what it is. In addition, most ill health is a result of stress. One of the best ways to de-stress is to relax, but many of us don't set aside the time to focus solely on ourselves.

So today, take some time to let go. Eliminate the things that aren't essential, and focus on what matters. As you quiet your mind, tune in to your body. Expand your awareness of what each part is experiencing. For example, really concentrate on your shoulders and note exactly how they're feeling. Is there tightness? A subtle throbbing? A dull feeling? Go through your entire body and "listen" to every part. Be sure to write everything down in your Process Journal.

Additionally, be aware of the physical reactions to the experiences you have today. Your body is *always* reacting to absolutely everything and sending you mes-sages, but you may not be consciously aware of these subtle second-by-second energy shifts. Ask yourself, *For me to physically feel this way, what might this indicate about my true feelings regarding the situation I'm in?*

Become a silent witness for a day. Take five minutes to be completely quiet. Do nothing. Think nothing. If a thought arises, imagine that it's a cloud drifting overhead, and let it float by. Be fully present with your body.

Level 2: Clutter-Clearing Your Identity

Your health is a direct result of your identity, which is the concept you have of yourself that you cart around through life. It's a jumble of beliefs, evaluations, opinions, rules, and perceptions about yourself and your body that serves as a filter through which you view every experience. If your filter contains thoughts that overweight people are unhappy, for instance, then everywhere you go, you'll see unhappy, overweight people. If *you* are overweight, then you'll certainly feel unhappy, *because this is what you believe.*

But is your "identity" really who you are? As Joseph Campbell said: "Am I the bulb that carries the light, or am I the light of which the bulb is the vehicle?" People who commit suicide offer interesting insight into this concept. A man who kills himself because his business fails has identified himself as his career. When his career fails, he feels that he fails. A woman who commits suicide because of a futile relationship identifies with the relationship; hence, when the relationship fails, she's believes that she's a failure. Likewise, a man who leaps off a bridge because he had lost a leg in an accident has identified himself as his body—thus, when his body is less, he is less (in his mind). A woman who runs into a burning building to save her jewels identifies more with her possessions than with her own body.

The challenge before you is that you may not be aware of even the smallest percentage of beliefs that make up your identity. Yet they are present at all times, dictating many aspects of your health, from the way your immune system responds to a virus to the manner in which your digestion reacts to various foods. Your beliefs are like air—they surround you, yet you usually aren't aware of them. Today, take time to examine your identity so that you can start to clear away anything that doesn't support your health and well-being. Try this exercise to help you become aware of exactly what your identity is.

Complete the following sentence in your Process Journal:

> "I identify myself with my [fill in the blank, such as job, children, possessions, home, ancestry, political party, relationships, reputation, body, or hair], and this affects my health in these ways: [insert all the ways that come to mind]."

Level 3: Clear Mental Clutter

Clear more clutter, especially if it relates to your body. For example, do you have piles of old medical-test results or doctors' bills that you could clear out? How about looking through your computer and deleting documents or saved e-mails that you no longer need or will even read again? Also clear out boxes of papers, old diaries, outdated files, and so on. Pay particular attention to anything that feels health related.

As you clutter-clear, pay attention to the thoughts that you have, on a consistent basis, regarding your body. Do they empower or diminish your body? If you wake up every morning repeating to yourself: *I have to lose weight. I look so fat. None of my clothes look good,* this becomes an affirmation and reinforces your belief that you look overweight and your clothes don't look good.

In addition, observe your inner or outer language regarding the way you refer to your body. Do you say, "*I'm* tired," or "*My body* is tired"? Ask yourself who or what is truly tired. When you aren't feeling well, do you say, "I'm sick," or "My body is sick"? Who or what is sick? (If your identity is strongly tied to your body, then as your body ages or is diminished in some way, you feel that *you* are old or diminished.)

Be conscious of the words you choose, especially regarding your physical self. Are they uplifting? Demeaning? Changing the way in which you speak can literally change the way you feel. When you catch yourself using language that lessens your body, immediately replace it with something reinforcing. You'll notice the difference! Here are some examples:

- "I'm exhausted" can become "My body is recharging."

- "I'm sick" can become "My body is taking some downtime."

- "I'm fat" can become "I'm a glorious, full-bodied woman."

Awareness is the first step. Does the language you use to describe your body bring you closer to your authentic self or take you further away from your source? Write down your observations in your Process Journal.

✢ ✢ ✢

Day 7

Hello!

Thank God for a new day! Something upsetting occurred yesterday, so I'm thrilled to be starting fresh. When I was clutter-clearing, I reached into a box and pulled out an old, tattered folder. The folder seemed to slip into my hands and something fluttered out. When I reached down and turned it over, I saw that it was a police photo of the gunman who shot me. (I was just a teenager at the time. It was a random shooting—I didn't know him.) There he was . . . just staring up at me. I shrieked and dropped the picture like a hot coal. The dogs didn't know why I screamed, so they dashed into the room in a frenzy, ready to protect me.

I didn't realize that I had this mug shot, so I was shocked to see it. Not wanting to take the time to burn it, I just ripped it up and threw it in the trash. I'm certain that it wasn't an accident that this occurred at this precise point in the 28-day program. After calming down, I thought about some of the beliefs I had adopted about my body at the time of this terrifying event. One was a result of what the doctors had told me: that I'd face health challenges for the rest of my life because of the severity of my injuries. I quickly jotted this down (and other negative beliefs) and crossed them out with a thick black pen. I then wrote new beliefs in my Process Journal. I know that the impact of those limiting beliefs on my health is now reduced.

Sending you immense love . . . always and forever,
Denise

Day 7 (Air): Exploring Your Body's Mission

There's a reason why you have your specific body. It's not an accident! From a spiritual perspective, this is the exact body you need for your mission on Earth. You may like it or dislike it. It may work perfectly, or it might have arrived "defective" and without a warranty, but it's the very best vehicle for the lessons you're learning. And there's a profound relationship between your purpose in the world and the body you've received. To the extent that your body and your mission are in alignment, there will be harmony in your life.

Affirmation for the Day

My body is enough, just as it is.

Today

Your body is always giving you messages about what's occurring within and around you. Continually tune in today, asking, *Body, what is your message for me right now?* (If you feel a sensation in a particular area, ask that area. If your shoulder aches, for example, ask your shoulder if there's anything you need to know.)

Reward
My reward for completing Day 7 is:

(Gift yourself this reward at the successful
completion of today's exercises.)

Overview

- *Committed to Change!*
  **Level 1: Create a Powerful Statement
  That Affirms Your Health**

- *Going for It!*
  Level 2: Why This Body?

- *Playing Full Out!*
  **Level 3: Make a Soul-Map Collage
  for Vitality and Health**

Level 1: Create a Powerful Statement That Affirms Your Health

Affirmations work to reprogram your subconscious
mind and can have an immediate effect on your body.
Here's a three-step method to create a *Power Affirmation*
that's a hundred times more commanding than an ordinary one.

Step 1: Create a positive health-related statement that feels incredible every time you say it. Start with the words *My body is . . .* Here's an example: *My body is filled with vigorous life-force energy!* When you invent your affirmation, make every word count.

Step 2: Say your Power Affirmation with passion, shouting out loud when you recite it. Repeat it over and over, but change the emphasis each time. For instance, say, <u>My</u> *body is strong!* The next time, shout, *My <u>body</u> is strong!* And then, *My body <u>is</u> strong!* Finally, *My body is <u>strong!</u>* By emphasizing different words, the affirmation won't become routine.

Step 3: Move your body. Punch the sky. Walk briskly. Dance. Stomp your feet as you shout out your affirmation with wild enthusiasm. When you do so, you create new neural pathways within your energy fields. Take at least five minutes to do your Power Affirmation.

Level 2: Why This Body?

Just as there's a reason why you incarnated at this particular time on the planet, there's also a reason why you chose the kind and type of body you have as well as your specific physical issues. When you understand why you chose your body (and its unique challenges), it helps bring clarity and focus into your life. Take some time to be still and ask yourself the following questions.

Write your answers in your Process Journal.

- *Why do I have my particular body?*
- *What do I learn from it?*
- *What do I gain from it?*
- *How might it serve me in the future?*

If you have difficulty answering these questions, imagine observing yourself as a stranger might. What judgments would a stranger make about your body? If that person had to decide which spiritual lessons there were for someone with a body such as yours, what would they be? For example, if you have a body that appears weak, a stranger might think that one of your lessons is to learn inner strength instead of outer strength. (Hint: What you believe that *others* think about you is usually an indication of your own subconscious beliefs about yourself.) Be sure to record your discoveries in your Process Journal.

Level 3: Make a Soul-Map Collage for Vitality and Health

If you knew the *purpose* of your particular body, what would it be? When you uncover the truth, a rush of energy fills you when you say it aloud *because the words resonate with your soul.* The words don't need to be fancy or eloquent—just real and authentic. If you don't feel that rush, you probably haven't found the deepest core purpose of your body.

On the back of a large poster board, write out the purpose of your body; on the front, make a collage that exemplifies it, as well as excellent health. Cut out pictures from magazines or print photos from the Internet to paste onto the board. Create the *feeling* of awesome, amazing health. You can also cut and paste words that describe the feelings you desire. You might use words such as *Vibrant! Toned!* or *Graceful!* Make sure that somewhere on the collage you put a photo of yourself. Create a Soul-Map Collage that feels incredibly alive, rejuvenated, and healthy.

Just looking at your collage should make you feel bursting with vitality. Put it in a place where you can see it often so that it can help you manifest your purpose and feelings of amazing health. You could copy or photograph it, and post the copies around your home or office. You could also laminate it or display it as your computer background. The more you see it, the better.

Reward
My reward for completing Air Week is:

(Gift yourself this reward at the successful completion of today's exercises.)

Your Accomplishments

Air Week has come to a close. Take a few deep, full breaths and reflect on what you have accomplished during the past seven days before shifting focus to Water Week. Write down your achievements and/or realizations in your Process Journal. Make sure that you reward yourself for completing Air Week! Congratulations!

CHAPTER TWO

Water Week— Clearing Your Emotional Body

I t's hot here today. *Really* hot! One of my greatest joys in this shimmering heat is our outdoor shower. It's open to the azure sky overhead and surrounded by a shoulder-high bamboo screen. Big, luscious palm fronds shade it in the blistering part of the day. When I turn the shower on, brisk cold water runs over my body and down my legs. It is so refreshing and renewing. There's something about being nude to the sky above, as chilly water cascades down over me, that rejuvenates my soul.

Water traditionally represents emotions, and this week is dedicated to purifying and cleansing the emotional self. Water also represents intuition, dreams, relationships, and childlike innocence and wonder. Our connection to water is primal—from allowing a waterfall to flow over our body, to swimming in a lake on a warm moonlit night, to waiting with outstretched arms to welcome a summer thunderstorm . . . the pleasure and deep meaning attached to our experiences of water is inspiring.

We begin life in water; and we're universally drawn to its soothing, cleansing, healing qualities. This deep attraction isn't hard to understand, given the fact that our bodies are mostly made up of water. Yet the water that flows within us didn't start its journey with our birth, and it will continue to flow after we die. That very same water has gently flowed down the golden Nile, it's been a mist high in the Himalayas, and it's even hung in a cloud over the Brazilian rain forest. Beyond the obvious need we have to hydrate our bodies, there is perhaps also an etheric memory stored within our genetic imprinting, which connects us to water (in all its forms) and reinforces our yearning to meld with it.

Throughout history, water has also represented purification and cleansing. One well-known example is India's holy river, the Ganges, which is revered by millions of Hindu pilgrims who bathe in it every day to spiritually cleanse and purify themselves.

This second week is dedicated to an in-depth purification and balancing of your emotional self. Releasing limiting emotions can help you unlock the secret messages of your body as well as strengthen your health. (People who have continual, low-level emotional stress tend to be more likely to have a cluster of risk factors, including elevated blood pressure, high triglycerides, low levels of HDL [good] cholesterol, abdominal obesity, and elevated blood sugar—all of which are basically steps on the road to heart attack or diabetes.)

The Next Seven Days

1. Choose Your Emotions

It's a myth that good people don't have negative emotions. However, emotions are only truly negative if you suppress them (or dump them on someone else). In many families and societies, people are encouraged to refrain from displaying how they feel. You may have heard that "real men don't cry," or "one should never get angry." What happens to the feelings that aren't expressed, though? Some have described it as wearing a backpack, and each time you suppress or stuff an emotion, it's like putting a small stone inside your pack. A few might not be a big deal, but if this occurs once a day, then over a year this could amount to more than 100 pounds. Carrying around extra baggage (unprocessed emotions) doesn't promote excellent health.

When you suppress what you're feeling, your emotions become trapped in your body tissues, which leads to illness, disease, or disharmony. You have the choice of processing your feelings or dragging them around with you. How do you wish to use your life-force energy: carrying a cumbersome backpack or enjoying a lightness of being in every moment? This week, say, "I choose to experience all my emotions." Whenever an emotion comes up, move into it rather than away from it. Feel it. Allow it, rather than deny it. Choosing *what is so* empowers your body by acknowledging exactly what's occurring within you right now. It's a path of healing.

2. Hydrate! Nourishing Your Body

During this week, drink plenty of water. This doesn't include sparkling or carbonated mineral water. Many health problems can be reduced or even eliminated if the body has enough fluid to cleanse and purify itself. You may think you only need to drink when you're thirsty, but usually by that time, you're already on the way to becoming dehydrated. Every person's intake needs are different, but one test is to pull the skin on the inside of your wrist. If it bounces right back when you release it, then most likely you've consumed enough water. If it doesn't, then you might need to drink more.

3. Expand Your Awareness of the Water Around You

From the water you splash on your face in the morning; to the water that percolates for your coffee; to the water that flushes your toilet and washes your clothes; to the water inside your body; to the waters in nature—the mist, rain, snow, oceans, lakes, and rivers . . . pay attention to the water that's all around you. Imagine that you're connecting to the Spirit of Water as you do so.

4. Cleanse

During the next seven days, be sure to cleanse your body and your environment. While you shower or bathe, say affirmations such as: *As I cleanse my body, I feel lighter, brighter, and full of life-force energy and vitality.* While you clean the floors in your bedroom or bathroom, say, *As I clean, my body is grounded and strong.* Eating lighter and healthier foods that include leafy greens and vegetables can also help cleanse your body.

In addition, try to do more clutter-clearing throughout your home. This week, clean out the spaces (after the clutter has been removed) before putting back the items that you love or use. Your body and environment are indeed closely connected. This is the time for inner and outer cleaning.

5. Share

As much as possible, share the emotions you experience this week with others, as it can have a powerful impact on your health. In a famous study at Stanford, women with late-stage breast cancer were divided into two groups. One group was given standard medical care, while the other group received standard care but also sat down once a week and shared their feelings about the disease. This produced remarkable results: the women who talked about their disease and discussed their feelings lived twice as long as the group who just received medical treatment. *They lived longer, simply by sharing their feelings.*

During Water Week

- Explore the connection between your body and emotions.

- Communicate from your heart, especially the things that you've been afraid to say.

- Drink lots of water.

- Examine your relationships—present and past—to discover the effects they've had on your health.

- Cleanse your body and your home.

- Look for links between your childhood and your current sense of well-being.

Day 8

Hi!

*Yippee! You made it to the second week! Congratulations!
Did you remember to write in your Joy Journal every day and celebrate what you <u>did</u> accomplish? Remember . . . you don't have
to do this program perfectly for it to work wonders.*

*It's never too late for a new beginning! We are entering
Water Week, which usually brings up emotional stuff for me-
and almost everyone who participates in the program. But after
the wild ride during Air Week, I feel like I've cleared so much out
that (hopefully) this coming week will be a breeze.*

*I took some time to look at what I <u>did</u> accomplish during Air
Week, and here's what I noted:*

1. *I wrote down what I ate every day.*

2. *I clutter-cleared my entire kitchen—every drawer, cup-
    board, and shelf!*

3. *I clutter-cleared the pantry, my office files, my diaries,
    a lot of photos, and my books. (I gave away boxes and
    boxes of stuff.)*

4. *I drank a lot less wine. (I usually have two glasses with
    dinner, but I cut back to less than one . . . and I didn't
    have any alcohol at a party where everyone else was
    drinking).*

*Wow! It's great to see what I <u>did</u> achieve over the past week.
If I hadn't taken the time to write it down, I wouldn't have realized how much I actually accomplished, and I might have still
been feeling like a failure. Actually, what I did do was substantial. (And if you take the time to reflect about last week, I bet it
was for you, too.)*

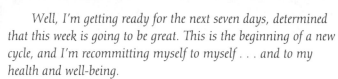

*Well, I'm getting ready for the next seven days, determined
that this week is going to be great. This is the beginning of a new
cycle, and I'm recommitting myself to myself . . . and to my
health and well-being.*

Good luck for this coming week, and heaps of love!

Denise

Day 8 (Water): Your Body Believes Every Word You Say

In no small way, your body believes every word you
say. The beliefs you hold about yourself and your life
can literally dictate the quality of your health. Everything
you say (or think) has an associated emotion and is constantly affecting your well-being.

Emotions are the juice of life, the filter through
which you view the world. They are your keys to knowing if something is right or wrong for you. They also
offer internal signals about what's occurring in your surroundings, letting you know if you're safe or if caution
is needed. Your emotions reflect the decisions and judgments you make about yourself and your body. They
also affect your health and the way you feel, for each
emotion is experienced as a bodily sensation. (For example, fear might be felt as a tingling in the shoulders,

a hot spot in the abdomen, or a restricted feeling in your chest.)

For today's exercises, you'll have the opportunity to begin exploring your beliefs (and their associated emotions) and pinpointing where each resides in your body.

Affirmation for the Day

I unconditionally accept my feelings about my body.

Today

Energize water before you drink it, either by holding your hand over the glass and imagining energy from your hand filling your glass, or by simply visualizing energy pouring down from the heavens and filling the glass.

Reward

My reward for completing Day 8 is:

(Gift yourself this reward at the successful completion of today's exercises.)

Overview

- *Committed to Change!*
  Level 1: Seven Great Things about Your Body!

- *Going for It!*
  Level 2: What Decisions Do You Make about Yourself Based on Your Body?

- *Playing Full Out!*
  Level 3: What Judgments Do You Make about Others (Based on Their Bodies), and What Do These Judgments Say about You?

Level 1: Seven Great Things about Your Body!

Your primary relationship is with your body—it goes through every experience with you. It's your permanent life companion, whether you like it or not. Your body could be your best friend and ally or your worst enemy. It's all up to you.

Your body listens to you. When you say positive things about it, it responds in kind. In this exercise, you'll focus on what's great about your body. In your Process Journal, write the heading "Seven Great Things about My Body," and then start listing them. Don't be shy! Blow your own horn here. Your body will believe what you say! Then every day (for the next seven days), add seven *more* things that you love about your body. Notice where in your body you sense the feelings or emotions associated with your words. Be aware if any old beliefs arise as you engage in this. (You *can* choose your beliefs about yourself. You aren't stuck with any negative ones that you may have been holding on to.)

Every day this week, starting today, stand in front of the mirror and read your growing list out loud. Imagine that you're talking to someone who feels supported, nurtured, and loved by the wonderful things you're saying to her. Note your emotions as you do so. Where in your body do you feel them?

Level 2: What Decisions Do You Make Based on Your Body, and What Are the Corresponding Emotions?

Go back through your life and find the times when you made decisions about who you are based on your judgments about your body. These may have been positive or negative. (For example, you might have decided that you weren't attractive to the opposite sex because you have small breasts or a misshapen penis.) Also explore your current beliefs about your body. Write these things down in your Process Journal. Try to recall where those ideas came from. (Did a family member tell you that? Your religion? The media? Society?) As you read each belief, *notice what the corresponding emotion might be.* Experience the emotion as fully as you can. Then travel into your body to observe where that emotion resides. Feel it more. You are now immersed in the totality of this belief. At this point, you don't need to change any of these beliefs—you're just becoming aware of them and where they live.

When you're finished, ask yourself the following about each belief:

- *Is this really true?*
- *Do I want to continue to hold this decision?*

Write down whatever answers come up for you. If you made the decision that you're physically weak, for example, ask yourself if it's really true for you. Or maybe you made the choice that you were artistic because someone once remarked that you have the hands of an artist. Ask yourself if you're willing to continue to carry this decision, and be honest in your answers.

Level 3: What Judgments Do You Make about Others (Based on Their Bodies), and What Do These Judgments Say about You?

Make a list of five people you like and five people you don't. (You don't have to know all of these people personally.) Next to each name, write down the decisions that you've made about them *based on their bodies.* After you've completed this, go through your notes and see if any of these judgments relate to you. (On a deep level they all do, but just notice what comes up for you as you do this exercise.) Know that you can change these judgments, and by doing so, your body will change (for it responds to your thoughts and judgments about it).

Day 9

Dear Fellow Soul Traveler,

We are now fully on the journey into Water Week. Don't be discouraged by any emotions that are coming up for you. It's normal. I've been close to sniffles myself, as I'm continuing to arrange and clutter-clear my photos. It's been such a bittersweet yet precious way to revisit my past. I find myself feeling a depth of love as I look at the photos of the people with whom I've shared my past. However, at times, there's also a kind of grieving. I'm paying particular attention to how my body responds to each person as I pick up another photo. Sometimes my body is giving me information that my mind isn't conscious of. For example, I looked a photo of a cousin with whom I thought I had a good relationship, but when I tuned in to my body, I noticed that my abdomen tightened and my shoulders were tense. When I went deeper into the feeling, all sorts of less-than-positive childhood memories were revealed. I realized that my relationship wasn't as good as I thought it was.

Even though I'm uncomfortable, I know that something is growing and emerging within me, so I'm cherishing every experience. Remember that no matter what's occurring on the surface of your life, beneath it things are releasing, healing, and expanding. "It's happening!"

With all my love as you continue on this journey,
Denise

P.S. Are you keeping your commitment for your daily action? You should be getting remarkable results from doing so. If you're not keeping your word, either recommit or make a new commitment that you absolutely will uphold in order to empower your body.

Day 9 (Water): Is This Who You Are?

Everything you put on your body affects your energy and aura. Wearing a silk blouse feels different from an acrylic top, for example. And your body may respond differently to natural essential oils than synthetic perfumes made from petrochemicals. Slipping on five-inch heels will affect your energy one way; and donning soft, flat shearling boots does so in another. Even silver and gold jewelry affect your energy differently.

Sometimes the effect of what you put on your body is psychological. You'll feel completely different if you put on your old torn sweat suit than the special dress you bought while you were on vacation in Paris. Wearing the scarf you picked up at the dollar store won't affect your energy fields in the same way as wearing the scarf your husband gave you on your first date. It all has to do with the love and memories that you associate with it.

Interestingly, color plays a role in your auric field, and research has shown that it has a psychological impact as well. Red stimulates your appetite, for example. And did you know that pink can be a relaxing color when you're feeling agitated; or that when you wear blue, your blood pressure goes down?

Not only does everything you use to adorn or cover your body affect the energy of your body, but it also radiates into the world a strong message about who you are. The message you send out mirrors back to you in many ways. If the idea that you convey says "I'm incredibly vibrant and radiant!" the world around you will support that sentiment and mirror it back to you, as if it were an absolute truth.

Your body can also help determine your destiny. Taking time to discover not just who you are now, but *who you would like to become in the future* (and what you'd like your health to be) and dressing *as if it were already true* can help propel you in the direction of your dreams. Today's exercises help you become even more conscious of what's affecting your energy fields.

Affirmation for the Day
My body is a sacred vessel for Spirit.

Today
Be aware of everything you put on your body, such as creams and lotions, nail polish, makeup, perfume, essential oil, clothing, shoes, ties, scarves, and jewelry. Notice how everything subtly changes your energy.

Reward
My reward for completing Day 9 is:

(Gift yourself this reward at the successful completion of today's exercises.)

Overview

- *Committed to Change!*
  Level 1: Cleanse Your Body

- *Going for It!*
  **Level 2: What Are Your Symptoms?
  What Is the Cause?**

- *Playing Full Out!*
  **Level 3: Does This Represent
  Who You Are?**

Level 1: Cleanse Your Body

Cleansing can be a mundane task, but if you employ the power of symbolic ceremony, it can be incredibly renewing. If you usually just give yourself "a lick and a promise" when it comes to personal bathing or showering, take the time today to thoroughly cleanse every part of your body. When was the last time you cleaned between your toes? Behind your ears? In your ears? Your back? Imagine that you're talking to each part of your body as you do so: *Hi, elbow! I haven't thought about you for a long time. Thank you for all of the flexion and extension you allow.* Acknowledge and thank each part as you lovingly clean it.

Affirm as you bathe and cleanse your body: *My body is absorbing life-force energy from the water through my pores.*

Level 2: What Are Your Symptoms? What Is the Cause?

Almost every physical symptom has its source in a belief or decision that you have about yourself and/ or your life. If you only attend to the symptoms, you might "fix" them, but unless you go to the source or cause, it's likely to return either in the same form or a different one. List any symptoms that you have now (or have experienced in the recent past). Take a moment to be still, and ask yourself: *If I knew the source of this symptom, it would be . . .*

Perhaps you've been having pain in your feet, which makes it difficult to walk or stand. Write down the symptom: *painful, swollen feet.* After you tune in, you may discover that the cause of this condition is being afraid to step forward into a new venture. Or maybe you're hesitant to make a stand in life. There are no right answers—just what's correct for *you.*

There is always a place deep within that absolutely knows the cause of your every ailment. Oftentimes when you attend to the cause (for example, by taking the risk to step forward into a new area, if that is the message you get from your feet), the ailment and the symptoms disappear forever.

Level 3: Does This Represent Who You Are?

What you put on your body can help determine your destiny. It can change the way you feel about yourself, and this can change the way you relate to the world. It can also dramatically affect how your body feels physically. As you sort through your closet, notice if your clothes reflect who you are. Try on some outfits, and stand in front of a mirror. Ask yourself, *Does this reflect who I am? Does it represent who I desire to be?* Do the same with anything you wear on your body, such as scarves, jewelry, and watches. If you have any tattoos, ask yourself: *Do these symbols represent who I am? Do they represent who I desire to be?* If they don't (but you don't want to have them removed), ask yourself this: *How can I change the meaning that I ascribe to these tattoos?*

As you go through everything you put on your body, think about what decisions or judgments you'd make about someone else who might wear those particular kinds of clothes, jewelry, and shoes. Are you happy to be that person? Do your clothes convey to you and the world that you are vibrant, healthy, and toned? Write down all of your reactions in your Process Journal. If you need to do any clutter-clearing or reorganizing in your closet, this is the time to do so.

‡ ‡ ‡

Day 10

Hi!

You've made it to Day 10! That's fantastic! You're getting remarkable results, even if you aren't consciously aware of them. And when you're not actively <u>doing</u> the program, you're still <u>on</u> the program. Once you start a process of self-discovery, the forces of your life propel you in the direction of your destiny. So even if you miss a day or don't do everything "right," this is still working in your life.

Today I really had to remind myself that it was a Water Day and that everything that happened was all a part of the process. David (my husband) woke me up sometime after midnight to let me know that one of the dogs had diarrhea and that both dogs had tracked it all over the house. (Frankly, I think this could have waited until morning.) I couldn't get back to sleep, and in the early morning hours, I found myself—between gagging—scrubbing the floor first with soap, then vinegar, and then hand-washing the dogs' bedding. (Whew! I was scrubbing with lots and lots of <u>water</u> and then scrubbing myself, even between the toes, to clean it all off of me!) As I cleaned, I used this as a metaphor for releasing all the s--t that I no longer needed in my life.

As you continue on this journey, love, cherish, and accept yourself—and forgive yourself if it's not all done "perfectly." Doing this program perfectly isn't the purpose of it. Know that you will get results, no matter what you do (or don't do) between now and the end. No matter where life takes you in the next 18 days, the universe is working in powerful and mysterious ways to connect you more deeply with your soul.

All my love,

Denise

Day 10 (Water): What Are Your Energy Zappers and Juicers?

In every moment, your body is responding to the world around you in subtle (and not-so-subtle) ways. The colors and vibrancy of your auric field are constantly changing. When all is well, your aura is sparkling and bright; and when it isn't, the colors are dull and dim. Even if you can't see your aura, you can still feel what's taking place in your body. If you feel out of sorts, that is a message. Either you're eating the wrong kinds of foods, drinking or eating too much, breathing pollutants, going in the wrong direction in life, thinking the wrong kinds of thoughts, or spending time with the wrong people. All of these could (and do) affect your health and well-being.

When your body doesn't feel quite right, it's telling you that something is wrong. Most people are only aware of their body's messages when they realize they don't feel well and aren't attuned to the early warning signs. Today's exercises will help you begin to understand what your body is trying to tell you at all times. The challenge is to be able to tell what's enlivening your energy and what's depleting it before it's too late to make changes without a lot of effort.

The following exercises will help you discover the people, patterns, and foods that deplete or zap your energy, and those that uplift or "juice" your energy. The soul loves the truth, so when you identify your zappers, they have less of an effect on you. And when you focus on the juicers, you can expand their presence in your life.

If something or someone is an energy zapper for your body, take action today to minimize or eliminate this from your life. For example, if every single time you drink a milkshake you feel bloated and sleepy, it's probably a zapper. Alternatively, if you feel fantastic after hearing a particular song, this is a juicer. Today is about increasing your physical juicers and diminishing your zappers.

Affirmation for the Day

My body is in harmony with everyone and everything in my universe.

Today

Notice the relationship you have with every person and object you encounter. Does your body feel comfortable and strong or uncomfortable and weak? Does your physical energy go up or down— or is it neutral—with each person and object?

Reward

My reward for completing Day 10 is:

(Gift yourself this reward at the successful completion of today's exercises.)

Overview

- *Committed to Change!*
  Level 1: Identify Your Energy Zappers

- *Going for It!*
  Level 2: Find Out What Juices Your Energy

- *Playing Full Out!*
  **Level 3: Commit to Diminishing One Zapper
  and Increasing One Juicer**

Level 1: Identify Your Energy Zappers

Do you find that there are some people who zap your energy? Does other people's negativity impact your health? Do you feel like you've packed on pounds as a way to shield yourself from others? Are you a psychic sponge that absorbs the emotions of everyone around you? Is your body in a constant state of vigilance and hence always tense (also as a form of defense)? Some people create buffers around themselves as a form of psychic protection, but there are better ways to do this that won't impact your body. An energy zapper is anything that lowers your energy, thus decreasing your life force. Often you become so used to living with these zappers that you're not even conscious of their effect on you. Just becoming aware of them will begin to diminish their power. Throughout the day, notice what brings your energy down. Some examples might be:

- Sitting at your computer all day without taking breaks

- Always trying to please everyone

- Not drinking very much water

- Always feeling exhausted after having been with a particular person

- Spending much of the day in fluorescent-lit rooms with no windows

- Denying/suppressing what you are feeling

- Working without taking time off to rest and rejuvenate

- Watching excessive television

- Drinking too much alcohol

Write a list of your zappers in your Process Journal, and look for ways to eliminate or diminish some of them.

Level 2: Find Out What Juices Your Energy

It's equally important to discover the things that uplift your energy. What "juices" you? Write it down in your Process Journal. Here are some examples:

- Drinking hot tea while watching the sunrise
- Eating fresh fruits and vegetables
- Going for a walk

- Doing yoga
- Working in the garden
- Getting eight hours of sleep a night
- Snuggling under the covers with a great book
- Spending time with friends

Read through your list of juicers, and see if there are any ways you can increase or expand them in your life.

Level 3: Commit to Diminishing One Zapper and Increasing One Juicer

List the current activities in your life—that is, think about what you do on a regular basis from the time you wake up until you go to sleep. (This is where the pie chart—the one you created before the program started— might be helpful.) Close your eyes and visualize yourself doing each activity, and notice how your body feels. Do you seem to feel more energy and vitality, or do you feel drained and exhausted? Some activities might be neutral—in other words, they don't bring your energy up or down.

Now go through your list again, and on a scale from 0 to 10 (where 0 is a real zapper, 5 is neutral, and 10 is a real juicer), give each activity a number.

Make a commitment to change at least one zapper. For example, if watching excessive television depletes your energy, commit to reducing your time in front of the tube. So if you watch 21 hours of TV every week, cut back to 10, and decide what you're going to do with the 11 remaining hours that will *juice* your energy. You might decide to take a night class, try out a new hobby, read, or paint. Follow through on your commitment. Take action! The small steps you take aren't inconsequential. Ultimately, they can add up to being the very things that mattered.

Day 11

Hi!

Whew! What is it about Water Week?! I feel like I'm back to square one today with lots of self-defeating thoughts. I do know that powerful changes are occurring beneath the surface, even though I feel like I'm wading through molasses right now. A bright spot came when I received a card from a dear friend (which I immediately stuck right next to my computer). The front cover has a darling little happy ducky who's saying: "Sometimes life is all sunshine and rainbows!"

And when you open it up, it says, "Other times, it's just a steaming pile that won't flush. . . . (In any case, I'm there for you, amigo.)"

It was the perfect card for me because today was definitely not "sunshine and rainbows." (Maybe everything is getting stirred up because I'm still going through so many memories. I've thrown away tons of old photos today; in fact, I couldn't lift the box and had to get help just to shove it out the door—and I'm <u>still</u> not done.)

On the positive front, one of my canaries laid an egg today (which I accidentally crushed). Okay, so maybe it wasn't that positive. And on another (kind of) positive note, I finally took care of <u>all</u> the residual dog diarrhea. (Who would have guessed that one dog had so much poop stored up in him?!) Everything was cleaned, the couch covers were washed, and all of the floors were scrubbed again. Hopefully, this chapter in my life is complete.

Anyway, I sure hope that your day was "sunshine and rainbows" and not a "steaming pile."

With all my love . . . always,

Denise

Day 11 (Water): Exploring Your Relationship with Your Body

The way we know we exist is through our relationships. We have a relationship with our mother and father when we're born; then later on with other family members, friends, and co-workers. We also have a relationship with animals, the elements of nature (rocks, sky, rain, fire, and so on), and with the Creator. We even have relationships with objects (our car, computer, and food) and with money. And the most intimate relationship we have is with our bodies.

The way you relate to your body is a reflection of the way you relate to the world around you . . . and it reflects the way the world relates with *you*. Most important, the way that you relate with your body has a huge effect on your health.

Affirmation for the Day

*I love my body deeply and fully . . . and
I accept and appreciate it exactly as it is.*

Today

Choose another area of your home to clean. Remember that cleaning creates a fresh space that allows you and your body to feel lighter, brighter, uplifted, and more at peace. It allows space for your dreams to flourish! There's a very close connection between your inner and outer environments. While you clean, say affirmations, such as: *As I clean, I am creating space for even more vitality to fill my body.*

Reward

My reward for completing Day 11 is:

(Gift yourself this reward at the successful completion of today's exercises.)

Overview

- *Committed to Change!*
  Level 1: How Do You Relate to Your Body?

- *Going for It!*
  Level 2: Examine the Recurring Ways in Which You Relate to Your Body

- *Playing Full Out!*
  Level 3: What Does Your Body Want You to Know?

Level 1: How Do You Relate to Your Body?

When you begin to examine your relationship with your body, you may find that the way you connect with your body is a reflection of the way others treated you when you were a child. For example:

- If your parents were critical of you, you may have a tendency to be very critical of your body.

- If you were ignored as a child, you may have a tendency to ignore your body.

- If you weren't allowed to communicate how you felt as a child, it's not uncommon for you to ignore the communications (of discomfort, and so forth) from your body.

- If your parents used harsh corporal punishment on you, you may have a tendency to (subconsciously) be drawn to situations in which your body is physically damaged.

- If your parents treated you with tremendous fear every time you were ill or injured, then you may find yourself reacting fearfully to sensations from your body.

Your parents, however, are not to blame. They related to you in the ways in which their parents related to them (and so on through the generations). The way you relate to your body is usually:

- A projection or mirror of the qualities that you suppress or don't accept within yourself

- A reflection of the way people related to you when you were young

- A reflection of the core beliefs that you have about bodies in general or about your particular body

Think about how you relate to your body, and write down your observations in your Process Journal. Taking time to examine this relationship helps you understand and unweave negative patterns that might be damaging your health.

Level 2: Examine the Recurring Ways in Which You Relate to Your Body

The way you relate to your body can come from your inner rules about life, but inner rules are just thoughts, and thoughts can be changed! For example, do you have an inner belief that you shouldn't show your anger to people who are rude, insensitive, or hurtful to you? Do you just ignore the increasing tightness in your shoulders and neck, and walk away (frustrated or resentful) rather than saying anything to that person? Every time you do so, you're damaging your body because you're treating it as if it mattered less than the feelings of another person. If you wouldn't treat a friend this way, you shouldn't treat your body in this manner, either.

If a bully confronts you, do you get stunned into silence, only to have your body tense up later as you think of all the things you could have said? Perhaps you developed an inner rule in childhood that silence is the best defense for any type of antagonism. When someone is humiliating you or being overly sarcastic, do you immediately become 7 years old instead of 50, and keep you mouth shut? Perhaps this would be all right, except that your physical self takes the brunt of your unwillingness to stick up for yourself, especially if this is a recurring theme in your life.

In a different vein, maybe you have an inner rule about not disappointing people. I knew someone who married a man she didn't love because she was so worried about disappointing his family (who had helped plan the wedding). Not long after they got married, this woman was diagnosed with cancer, and she told me that she saw a direct correlation between her inner rule about not disappointing people and the disease. In other words, her self-imposed rule had caused severe damage to her body.

Do you say *yes* whenever someone asks you for a favor, even when you'd rather say *no* at times? Or do you spend an inordinate amount of time trying to think of just the right excuse (rather than just speaking your truth), and then feel exhausted afterward? If so, your inner rule may be negatively affecting your body. Again, remember that your inner rules are only thoughts, and thoughts can be changed. What limiting inner rules are you willing to start to change today?

Level 3: What Does Your Body Want You to Know?

Allow yourself to go into a deep relaxed state, and then imagine that you're visiting each area of your body and talking to the Guardian of that area. Be sure to give the Guardian a persona. For example, the Guardian of your liver might look like a squatting dwarf with a red hat on his head. You might address him with respect, asking if he has any information for you regarding this organ. Listen to his reply, and write it down in your Process Journal.

If you receive advice from some of the Guardians, consider following it. The exercise below is one of my secret healing techniques, which has enabled me to over-come huge physical challenges in my life. (A Hawaiian shaman first taught me this method almost 40 years ago. She said that it was an ancient healing technique.)

How to Find the Message

Your body talks to you every day, but if you're too busy, you can't hear what it's trying to say. Whether or not you're conscious of it, your body is always commu-nicating with you. Use this day to begin to hear—even more—its heartfelt messages. If there's a specific area that's in discomfort or ill health, or if you're working to change different aspects of your body, take some time to review the following questions (and write the answers in your Process Journal).

Regarding your physical condition:

1. Where is the sensation in your body that seems to be (or could be) associated with this condition?

2. If it had a color, what would it be?

3. If it had a size, how big or small would it be?

4. If it had a shape, what would it look like?

5. If it had a texture and/or temperature, what would it be?

6. If there were emotions, attitudes, or feelings associated with this area, what would they be?

7. If there were memories from the past (this life or a past life), what would they be?

8. If there was a message, what would it be? Do you need to take any action?

❦ ❦ ❦

Day 12

Hi!

You're well into Water Week, so don't be concerned if many emotions are surfacing. Just allow them to rise and flow through you . . . the way a great river flows to the sea.

Something remarkable just happened to me, which brought up lots of sweet emotions. I was in town—Paso Robles, California—hoping to catch a glimpse of Lance Armstrong as he crossed the finish line in the Amgen bike race. I stood on my tiptoes for almost 30 minutes trying to see through the crowd, waiting for the bicyclists to arrive. But just as I spotted Lance, someone lunged in front of me, and I didn't see anything except the back of all of the spectators. However, that's not what brought up the emotions.

As I waited for the crowd to subside, I sat down on a bench in the park. A young man with Down syndrome asked if he could sit next to me, and I scooted over to make room for him. He plopped down, turned to me, and said, "I love you!" as he flung his arms around me in a big hug. He kept saying, "I love you! You're wonderful!" It was a simple, vulnerable expression of love . . . without fear or judgment. It felt holy and healing, and I was deeply touched. To me it seemed like it was a part of the opening that occurs during Water Week.

All my love . . . always,

Denise

Day 12 (Water): Being Still / Doing Nothing

Remember that whether or not you're conscious of it, your body is *always* communicating with you. Continue to tune in and open yourself to hearing your body's wisdom.

Affirmation for the Day
In the center of my being, there is always stillness and peace.

Today
There is stillness even in the center of a cyclone. No matter what's going on around you, there is always an inner sanctuary of profound tranquility.

Reward
My reward for completing Day 12 is:

(Gift yourself this reward at the successful completion of today's exercises.)

<u>Overview</u>

- *Committed to Change!*
  Level 1: Go Slow

- *Going for It!*
  Level 2: Watch for Signs

- *Playing Full Out!*
  **Level 3: Do Nothing . . .
  Dissolve into Nothingness**

Level 1: Go Slow

We often go so fast in life that we're out of touch with what we're really experiencing. But when we slow down, it's much easier to stay attuned with what's authentic.

Today, choose one physical activity (such as eating, walking, or breathing), and *slow it way down*. Spend 15 minutes "going slow." If you choose eating, for example, take your time chewing, and cherish every nuance of flavor and texture. Be aware of the way your teeth and tongue work together, the way the food flows from your mouth into your stomach, and how your body immediately begins to utilize the nutrients.

Level 2: Watch for Signs

In every moment, the universe is whispering to you. Take time today to watch for signs that are occurring around you, and check in with yourself to see if there are any messages from your body. There is often a correlation between outer signs and the inner workings of the body. For instance, if your sewer backs up, this could be a reflection of the need to do some bowel cleansing of your own. (Or it could just be a backed-up sewer.) When something occurs, ask yourself, *If this were saying something about my body, what might it be?*

Dedicate some time during the day to just "be" with your body. Sit quietly and allow yourself to fully tune in to what your body is feeling. *Experience what your body is experiencing.* Most people get so caught up in their day-to-day lives that they don't actually know what their bodies are experiencing. Some individuals are so alienated from their body that they're lucky their head is connected to it.

Today, imagine that your body is a very dear friend whom you haven't seen for a long time, and just "be" present with her (or him). Listen to what she has to say. Be present with your breath. Be present with the rhythm of your heart. Be present each time you blink your eyes. It's a holy thing to truly be in the moment with another, so for today, *be present with your body.*

Level 3: Do Nothing . . . Dissolve into Nothingness

We get pulled into the hectic activity of life; and we also get drawn into the inner tangle of our constant thoughts, judgments, and evaluations. It takes a certain amount of courage to do nothing! In fact, it can be quite a challenge to simply sit still.

Rest. Be. *Do nothing.* It can be one of the most difficult, courageous, and rewarding things a human being can do. Take at least one hour today to just be. As your body relaxes, let everything slow down. Focus on what you're hearing—take your time listening. Concentrate on what you're seeing; see slowly. Smell slowly. Tune in to what you're feeling physically and emotionally. Feel slowly. Then let it all go, and imagine that your body is dissolving into nothingness. (As a suggestion, you might want to do this exercise with ambient music.)

⚜ ⚜ ⚜

Day 13

Hi!

I'm over-the-moon happy today . . . and for no good reason. It's great! The emotions that come to the surface at this stage aren't just ones that make you feel uncomfortable. Although during the last few days you might have felt sadness, grief, anger, stress, or fear, you also might have experienced joy, bliss, and exhilaration. (Usually by this time in Water Week, many people note that numerous emotions arise. This can be immensely beneficial for your health!)

All emotion is logged into the body, so today, whatever feelings you're observing—whether you call them positive or negative—try to experience them fully rather than ignoring, denying, or suppressing them. In other words, _choose_ to feel. For example, maybe you feel fearful today. Perhaps, for you, fear is a tight feeling in your chest. So instead of trying not to feel it, feel it more. Create even more constriction in your chest, and feel as much "fear" as you can. Exaggerate it. Choose to feel it! (And you can do this with positive emotions as well.) Magnify every emotion that arises today.

I know this might sound very strange, but when you do so, a remarkable thing can happen as a result. As soon as you _do_ a "negative" emotion rather than have it "done" to you, it becomes less worrisome. Tell yourself: "I'm doing fear," "I'm doing sadness," "I'm doing worry," and so on. You can also do a so-called positive emotion: "I'm doing joy!" "I'm doing bliss!" It can actually be fun—try it. When you do your emotions, then _you_ are in control. This, in turn, dramatically empowers your health.

All my love,

Denise

Day 13 (Water): An Attitude of Gratitude

One of the fastest ways to empower and energize our bodies is to surround ourselves with an attitude of appreciation. We get so busy in our lives that we forget to be thankful for all that we have and all that we are, yet gratitude is a key to health and happiness.

What you focus on in life is what you create. When you focus on what you're grateful for, you bring more of those things into your life. And when you focus on what you lack, you send a strong message to the universe that you're lacking, which becomes a self-fulfilling prophecy. By concentrating on how much you truly appreciate your body and health, miracles abound.

Affirmation for the Day
*I am blessed with a remarkable body,
and I am so grateful.*

Today
Focus on different parts of your body,
and focus on great things about each part.

<u>Reward</u>

My reward for completing Day 13 is:

(Gift yourself this reward at the successful
completion of today's exercises.)

Overview

- *Committed to Change!*
  Level 1: Have Gratitude for Your Body!

- *Going for It!*
  **Level 2: Be Thankful for the Things You
  Aren't Grateful For**

- *Playing Full Out!*
  Level 3: "I Love You. I Appreciate You."

Level 1: Have Gratitude for Your Body!

From the moment you read this until you go to
sleep, focus on what's good about your body. Be sincere.
Experience how your body responds to your heartfelt
appreciation.

Level 2: Be Thankful for the Things You <u>Aren't</u> Grateful For

Think about the things that you're grateful for regarding your body, and write them down in your Process Journal. Then make a list of the things you're *not* grateful for so that you can take each one and try to find a way that you could be more appreciative of it. For example, you might write: "I'm not grateful for my failing eyesight." But when you think about it, without your diminished sight, perhaps you wouldn't be taking the time to concentrate on your other senses. Maybe you notice that you hear things you've never heard before or smell things you've never smelled before. So cross it out, and write: "I'm grateful for my failing eyesight because it has allowed my other senses to expand. Now I can experience the world in ways I never have before."

Level 3: "I Love You. I Appreciate You."

There's a direct correlation between your willingness to love your body and the vibrancy of your health. A body that is truly loved vibrates with life-force energy. The energy of a body that is hated or despised shrivels, and the aura becomes gray and lackluster. Today, stand in front of a mirror, look at your body, and say: "I love you. I appreciate you."

When I first tried this, it was extremely difficult. I had a hard time even standing in front of the mirror because I thought I looked so disgusting. To gaze at myself and say, "I love you, Denise," seemed like a big fat lie. And it was so embarrassing to be standing there talking to myself. So I started out by looking in the mirror and saying this to myself: *I am willing to <u>think</u> about loving you, Denise.* Somehow that didn't seem like a lie. I kept doing this exercise until I could finally say, "I love you, Denise."

Now there are even some mornings when I wake up, look at myself in the mirror, and say, "Hello, Gorgeous!" It's amazing how good it makes me feel. If you have trouble with this exercise, find the words that feel true to you and then keep practicing until you can finally say: "Hello, Gorgeous! I love you!"

Additionally, massage your body today. Using fragrant oil or lotion, take a substantial amount of time to lovingly tend to each and every part. You might start with your feet and move upward. As you focus upon each area, affirm how much you appreciate it. Show your gratitude to your body! (You might also wish to schedule some professional massages during this program.)

D a y 1 4

Hi!

    We are almost halfway there . . . and it's never too late to begin anew. No matter what you accomplished (or didn't accomplish) on this program already, you can view today as a fresh start. Know that amazing results can occur in an instant. Any moment can be a turning point regarding your health.

    As a young woman, I lived in a Zen Buddhist monastery for several years. The Zen master, Yamada Roshi, told us that enlightenment could happen in an instant; however, he also said that if we thought it would take a long time—and a lot of effort—it would. But if we believed that it <u>could</u> happen instantly, then it was possible. (Okay, I lived there for over two years and never got "enlightened," but lots of other wonderful things occurred. To tell you the truth, at the time I believed that it would take 20 years to achieve enlightenment, so no wonder it never happened.)

    Sometimes people embark on this health program and think they need to spend a lot of time and effort to achieve something substantial. It's true that if you put in lots of effort, you'll get results . . . but it doesn't have to happen that way. No matter how you do this program, you <u>will</u> get results. Don't be concerned if things are working out differently from what you expected. Please know that <u>all is unfolding exactly as it should.</u>

    Be willing to let go of expectations about the ways in which this program must evolve for you to get results. Recommit yourself. Celebrate what you <u>have</u> accomplished in the last two weeks!

    Here at Summerhill Ranch, I'm still going through photos and mementos from the past and releasing so much of it. Today, I threw away all of the poems I wrote in high school. They sure were maudlin and morose. But as I read each one, I cherished the girl (me!) who wrote them, understanding why she felt the way she did.

    Love . . . always,

Denise

Day 14 (Water): Choosing Your Body

Today is the last day of Water Week. It's a day where you can make health choices that can have a huge impact on your well-being. Although it's common to think that changing an old pattern takes time, effort, and struggle, it can also occur in a flash. *The moment you make a choice with absolute certainty and clarity, while cutting off all other pathways, your life irrevocably changes forever.*

Affirmation for the Day
*Who I am is enough, and my body
is enough just as it is.*

Today

There is a direct correlation between the clarity in your home and the strength of your energy field. Find another area of your home to clean. Perhaps you could wash the windows, scrub the floors, dust the shelves, or wash the curtains. Do so with the intention of clearing your energy field so that it's brighter and more radiant as you clean.

Reward

My reward for completing Day 14 is:

(Gift yourself this reward at the successful
completion of today's exercises.)

Overview

- *Committed to Change!*
  Level 1: Ask Yourself "Noble Questions"

- *Going for It!*
  Level 2: Don't Blame Life for Your Health

- *Playing Full Out!*
  Level 3: Choose Your Body

Level 1: Ask Yourself "Noble Questions"

Did you know that much of self-talk is through questions? Some are mundane such as, *What will I make for dinner?* However, there are also disempowering ones like, *Why do I always eat so much?* These are called *unworthy questions.* If you ask yourself something negative, self-deprecating, or unworthy regarding your body, you'll damage your health over time. This kind of self-talk keeps you in victim mode.

Whenever you ask a negative question, the subconscious mind searches—almost like a computer—to find the answer. _It doesn't doubt the premise of your question; it just tries to find an answer._ So if you ask yourself, _Why do I always fail every time I try to lose weight?_ your subconscious will come up with a response, such as: _You fail because you don't deserve any better,_ or some other nonproductive answer. It assumes that you'll always fail because that is the premise of your question.

Whenever you catch yourself engaging in this, immediately replace the unworthy query with a noble one. For example, if you had asked, _Why am I always so tired?_ switch it with something like this: _How can I experience even more vitality?_ Your mind doesn't doubt the premise that you're _already_ experiencing vitality, so your body responds by feeling good! _Noble questions can be better than affirmations because they lead to action, and once you're in action mode, you'll feel like you're in control._

For today, create one inspiring, noble question to repeat over and over again. Some examples are:

- _How can my physical strength and vitality increase even more?_

- _How can I experience even greater health?_

- _How can I attain even more endurance?_

Level 2: Don't Blame Life for Your Health

Do you sometimes blame others or life in general for the challenges with your body? If you answered yes, then you're allowing yourself to be a victim. The truth is that you're never truly a victim—unless you *allow* yourself to feel that way. You *always* have the choice to step beyond feeling out of control or at the mercy of someone (or something) else. Even when it seems like you're a victim to the rest of the world, you can choose the meaning that you give the situation.

Remember that with enough motivation, you would indeed do whatever it took to invigorate, heal, and/or empower your body. *It is simply a matter of finding the right inspiration.*

If someone said to you, "I'll give you a million dollars in cash if you do absolutely everything possible to support your health for one month," you'd be going on power walks every morning, taking your vitamins consistently, and eating foods that supported your immune system. You'd do these things in a heartbeat. You would also jump into action if someone made an offer like this: "Look, I'll make sure that 100 children—who would have otherwise died of starvation—are given enough food and care so that they can live long into adulthood, *if* only you take care of your body for 28 days." If you knew that the well-being of others depended upon it, I guarantee that you'd do whatever it took to strengthen your body.

My point is that sometimes it's simply a matter of finding what drives you. Never mind if everyone in your family is overweight. Forget feeling like you don't have the time because you're so busy taking care of everyone else. Don't worry about the deep subconscious programming that may be keeping you from your goals. Big deal! Find your incentive. Find your motivation. Why is it essential that you strengthen your body? What might happen if you don't?

Level 3: Choose Your Body

You have a body. You might like it or dislike it, but it's yours for life. It's an act of power to consciously choose your body. I don't mean to just pick parts of it (such as the parts you like), but to choose all of it—every bump, wrinkle, vein, gray hair . . . *everything.*

You step into self-mastery when you *own* your body—this allows you to *be here now.* To be fully connected with your soul, it's valuable to accept the vehicle that houses it (your body) just as it is. This helps you stop living in the past so that you can be fully present here-and-now.

Tell the truth to yourself about your body, without judgment, criticism, comparison, hesitation, or denial. Then affirm: *I choose this body exactly as it is.* Keep saying this to yourself until you begin to feel unconditional acceptance of your physical self.

Even if deep down inside, you're kicking and screaming, shouting that you did *not* choose this body, choose it anyway. Maybe you're telling yourself that it was just the one that you were born with, or you really were an innocent victim of an accident that damaged it, or some other story. Know that just engaging in this exercise can help you step out of victim mode and into your majesty as a spiritual being with a vibrant, radiant body.

Reward
My reward for completing Water Week is:

(Gift yourself this reward at the successful completion of today's exercises.)

Your Accomplishments

Water Week has come to a close. Claim your end-of-the-week gift! Take a deep breath, and spend a few minutes reflecting upon what you've accomplished before you shift your energy to the tasks for the next seven days: Fire Week. Be sure to note your successes in your Process Journal. Rejoice in all that you are and all that you've achieved!

———— ⚱ ————

Chapter Three

Fire Week—
Clearing Your
Spiritual Body

Suddenly a loud explosion seemed to rock the house. David screamed, "Call 911!" I flew to the phone and dialed, as David yelled that the explosion had come from our neighbor's property across the road. Looking out the window, I could see flames soaring 25 feet into the air and catching big pine trees on fire. Minutes later we stood with our neighbors, who arrived at the same time as the fire trucks, and solemnly watched their home burn to the ground.

In that moment, all of our differences disappeared. (She wears high heels, I wear rubber flip-flops; he wears suits, David wears frayed jeans; they like to attend formal winemakers' dinners, we like to drink wine outside with our feet up on the picnic table.) Yet as we all watched the fire in disbelief, there was a common bond of humanity. We put our arms around each other and held one another in sadness. It was as if the fire had also consumed the barriers between us.

Fire has the ability to transform everything, and it's not an accident that in ancient cultures it's associated with Spirit for this reason. Here in the central coast of California, it's not uncommon to experience large forest fires, which dramatically level a landscape—yet every spring, there is life. Old brush is cleared away so that sunlight and moisture can reach the land to spur new growth.

It is during Fire Week that remarkable breakthroughs and transformations occur regarding old limiting patterns about your health. Don't be surprised if you experience powerful inner clearings during this time. Tapping into your natural radiance often entails facing the darkness of those limiting beliefs about your body.

This is also the week where you'll be asked to step out of your comfort zone and examine any attachment that you might have to keeping things exactly as they are. Also during the next seven days, you'll begin to take *massive action* to make a difference in your health. Get ready to step into expanded energy and vitality.

The Next Seven Days

1. Face Fear

In the first seven days of this program, you focused on clearing barriers that hindered your health. Usually the greatest blockage is fear, and this is the week when you'll be confronting this emotion. The fastest way to transform your body is through action, but it's easy to hesitate to make changes because of fear—fear of discomfort, of failure, of the unknown, and even of success. Fire Week is the time to look at your fears and *take action* to overcome them.

2. Become Aware of the Light Around You and Within You

This week deepens your awareness of the light that's around and within you. For example, become aware of the sunlight, noticing shadows and the interplay of brightness and darkness in your environment. Pay attention to the differences in indoor lighting, candlelight, and firelight. In a deeper sense, become aware of the inner light within you through the practice of meditation.

3. Change and Transformation

Fire represents change and transformation, so this is the time to take risks and try relating to your body in different ways. Be open to altering or modifying your routines and habits.

During Fire Week

- Step into the higher intelligence of your body with trust and faith.

- Connect with the innate wisdom within your cells.

- Use your body in new, creative ways.

- Activate an expanded identity through the way you move your body.

- Face any fear that might be lodged within your body.

- Dance your prayers.

✢ ✢ ✢

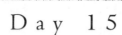

Day 15

Hi!

Holy cow! It's like the universe knows that we've started Fire Week . . . at least here at home in Summerhill Ranch. It was <u>hot</u> today! I was wearing rubber sandals and a thin T-shirt outside. I'm so glad to be into Fire Week! (It's my favorite element.)

If you've made it this far, the great news is that on this 28-day sojourn, you've turned a corner. If it hasn't happened to you yet, please don't be concerned. It's happening! Even when the ice on the surface of a river seems motionless, beneath it the water is flowing, and it won't be long until the ice starts to crack.

Hang on to your hat! Please don't despair, and keep going— please keep going! Something magnificent will occur.

With immense love and respect!

Denise

Day 15 (Fire): Releasing Fear from Your Body

On your journey to uncovering the mysteries of your body, it's valuable to explore the dark hidden crevices within your psyche for any submerged fears that are tucked away in your cells. *Every single fear that you have lodged in your body impacts your health!*

Stress is a modern-day code word for fear. If you experience constant stress, you're actually in a chronic state of low-level fear, which has been shown to have a damaging effect on the entire body. Often the thing that may be keeping you from stepping into full vitality and health are deeply hidden apprehensions. So it's valuable to face them head-on and bring them to the light of day.

Additionally, it's fear that tells you that you can't fully succeed in any health regime. (For example, maybe you're afraid of starting a new program because you're worried that, once again, you'll fail.) Fear can also keep you from trying something to empower your health, or it can keep you numb to the truth of what's really going on in your body. Fear blocks your exuberance and life force.

To step into a new relationship with your body, it's often necessary to understand and *own* your fears. In this way, they have less power. Suppress your fears and they become stronger; but if you acknowledge their presence and even lovingly accept them, they'll relinquish their hold on your life and body. Have faith that everything is unfolding as it should.

Affirmation for the Day
My body is safe.

Today

Activate your awareness of Fire. Be aware of all the forms of this element in your life—from the sun, to candlelight, to raging flames, and to the inner light within you. Imagine breathing in the energy of the sun's powerful rays, as every cell in your body becomes enlivened.

Reward

My reward for completing Day 15 is:

(Gift yourself this reward at the successful completion of today's exercises.)

Overview

- *Committed to Change!*
  Level 1: Bring Your Fears to the Light of Day

- *Going for It!*
  Level 2: Face Your Fears Regarding Your Body

- *Playing Full Out!*
  Level 3: Take Action!

Level 1: Bring Your Fears to the Light of Day

Fear in any form can zap your energy. When you acknowledge what you're afraid of, you take power away from this emotion, which has a strengthening effect on your body.

No fears are better or worse—they're just fears, and they're *not* who you are! In your Process Journal, list the things that you're afraid of regarding your body. At the top of a page, write: "I'm afraid of . . ." and be as specific as possible. (For example, perhaps you're afraid of getting old, losing your eyesight, never being in shape, getting cancer, becoming grossly overweight, becoming incontinent, being crippled, getting Alzheimer's, or not living up to your physical potential.) Write it all down! Taking time to name your fears can loosen the hold that they have over you.

Level 2: Face Your Fears Regarding Your Body

After you've written your list, choose your biggest fear and *imagine* (or visualize) a worst-case scenario regarding it. Then find a way that you could survive *and even thrive* if this were to happen to you. (I know this might be hard.) Keep doing this exercise until you get to the place where you can look your biggest fear and gleefully shout: "So what!" You have to be very creative in this exercise, but keep going until, for example, you can say: "So what! I have cancer! Ha, ha, ha!" "So what! I have to wear a hearing aid! Ha, ha, ha!" "So what! I'm as big as Texas! Ha, ha, ha!"

The truth is that *you are not your body.* The more that you can face changes or imbalances within it with grace and acceptance, then the more likely you are to move into an even deeper mastery of your body. And at that point, you'll be able to truly enjoy your body . . . no matter what shape it's in. Resistance causes distress; trust and surrender lead to transcendence and vibrancy.

Level 3: Take Action!

One of the most important things you can do to change the quality of your health is to take action. You already know what's working (or not working) regarding your body. You've read health books, listened to lectures, and watched TV talk shows—you know what you need to do. *But knowing what to do is not enough!* Today, your goal is to take substantial action steps. Begin now!

Start off by asking yourself, *What can I do right now to become stronger, healthier, and more vibrant?* Then whatever inner advice comes up for you, do it (even if it seems silly or small). Take some kind of action—any kind—right now in the direction of your goals. At this moment, you could do ten push-ups, for example, or take five deep breaths, or stretch your arms over your head. There are thousands of different things you could do to make a positive difference. Action builds momentum. Any action is better than none at all. *Just do it!* Right now!

‡ ‡ ‡

Day 16

Hi!

Fire energy ignites excitement, change, and transformation. Don't be dismayed if excitable emotions come up this week, such as anger, irritation, and frustration. It's not bad if they do arise, as they're coming to the surface in order to be examined. If you're feeling fabulous, don't think that it's not working; just enjoy it! Everyone processes these exercises differently.

Remember that once you've committed to the program, the universe works in mysterious ways to move you in the direction of your goals. For example, today I was thinking that I really needed to improve my memory. Then out of the blue, a friend gave me some supplements that she said had an amazing effect on the brain. I don't think this was a coincidence!

Once you embarked on this program, spiritual forces gathered to propel you forward, regardless of whether or not you were consciously directing it. You're being guided throughout this journey . . . even if it seems that on some days you barely think about the program. You're still on it—and it's working! Believe.

All my love . . . always and forever,
Denise

Day 16 (Fire): Taking Risks and Expansive Self-Love

If you do what you've always done, you'll get what you've always gotten. In other words, if everything stays the same, nothing changes. Regarding your health and your body, if you continue down the same path yet expect different results, you may be waiting for quite a while. It's time to change the way you've been thinking about your well-being. What would you do if your health was absolutely incredible? What would you experience? How would your life change?

Dr. Lawrence LeShan, who works with cancer patients, wrote that when a patient comes in, he asks them what they want to live for. He reports that most of the answers fall into three categories:

1. The first category is a result of fear. These patients want to live because they're afraid of death and the pain of dying, or they're afraid of not knowing what will happen after they die.

2. The second group wants to live for someone else. They want to live for their kids or their husband or their parents.

3. The third category—which is much smaller than the first two—are those who want to live because they wish to sing their own song, to experience all that they can be. (This is what I call *expansive self-love.*)

Dr. LeShan reports that of the three groups, it's the third that's much more likely to survive and thrive. These individuals want to live, not because of fear or for the sake of others, but because they want to embrace and cherish themselves and life in its fullest.

Masaru Emoto, an author and researcher, has conducted experiments showing how speech and thought directed at water (before it's frozen) creates ice crystals that are beautiful or ugly, depending on whether the projected sentiments were positive or negative. Since we are largely made up of water, perhaps we can affect our own body's water by our choice of speech and thoughts.

You've probably noticed that you feel great when you receive a compliment but feel down when someone makes a negative remark about you. *You* have a similar effect on your body. As you love yourself and your life, you're infusing all the water and cells of your body with life-force energy and vitality!

Why do you want to get in shape, heal a chronic condition, lose weight (or whatever your concern may be)? This is an important question. Do you want to do so because you're afraid of the consequences if you don't, or the judgments that others will make about you? Do you want to become healthier for your family, your kids, or your spouse? Do you wish to heal yourself because it will give you the freedom to experience life more fully and with more ease?

Think about this and be honest. The people who are most likely to enhance their health do it from a place of wanting to experience life *even more fully*—and having a body that allows flexibility and freedom of movement can help them attain this—rather than from a fearful place or wanting to please others. If you've had challenges making changes to your body, you need to be willing to do things differently. Be open to taking some risks and trying something new.

<u>Affirmation for the Day</u>

*I am free to experience joy in my body . . .
no matter what is happening in my life.*

<u>Today</u>

Constantly ask yourself the *noble* question: *How can I experience even more joy today?* See what your subconscious comes up with!

<u>Reward</u>

My reward for completing Day 16 is:

(Gift yourself this reward at the successful completion of today's exercises.)

<u>Overview</u>

- *Committed to Change!*
  Level 1: Have Fun!

- *Going for It!*
  Level 2: Step Out of Your Comfort Zone

- *Playing Full Out!*
  Level 3: The Law of Reversal

Level 1: Have Fun!

Ask your body what it would like to do that would be *fun* for it. Really, I'm serious—have a talk with your body. You can do this in a mini-meditation. If your body says, *I'd love a pedicure,* give it one. Or if it says, *I'd like to lie down for five minutes with my feet up,* then do that. Perhaps it might say, *I'd like to sit in the demo massage chair at the store!* Hey, think about doing it!

The next exercise involves taking a risk, but it's one of the fastest ways to stimulate your immune system: Laugh yourself silly! Don't just giggle; laugh with the exuberance of a child. Even if you don't really feel like it, pretend to have a huge belly laugh. Guffaw. Snort. When was the last time you had a cackling, chortling, fall-down-laughing fit? Never?! Why not start today? Even faking it can have an amazing impact on your soul. Come on. Really do it! You have nothing to lose . . . and everything to gain. (Lots of research promotes the idea that even a few minutes of laughing—even if it's forced—can have a powerful positive effect on your immune system.)

Level 2: Step Out of Your Comfort Zone

Have you ever had a pair of old shoes that were so worn in that they were easy to slip into at any time? They might have been totally out of style, had holes in the soles, zero arch support, and the seams were tearing apart; but they were familiar and oh so comfortable. New shoes—even if they are much better for your feet and made from the best-quality materials—may still pinch and feel stiff. They just aren't broken in like your old pair, so it's hard to wear them. And just like new shoes, sometimes it's not easy to make changes, even if doing so would improve your health.

But today is the day to take a step out of your comfort zone. I've heard of studies where cancer patients were asked to completely change their routines, hairstyles, clothing, and so on—all of which deeply shifted the way they saw themselves and life, because they stepped away from their identity as cancer patients. *Remarkably, there were much higher levels of spontaneous remission in this group than in the test group.* The theory is that their outer changes affected their inner selves.

So make a change for today. Surprise people! Surprise *yourself!* Be unpredictable—move your body differently. Walk barefoot in the snow . . . heck, roll in it and throw handfuls in the air. Avoid the path of least resistance!

Walk backward up the library steps. Light some candles, and sensuously dance naked. Do something (anything!) that is out of character for your body. Break some habits.

When you make transitions in life, you *must* leave your comfort zone, travel through a period of uncertainty, and finally arrive at a new beginning. Sometimes it will feel like one step forward and one backward. Breaking out of your self-imposed routine can help you dispel any "solidifying" of your identity that keeps you from renewing your body.

In a way, this is a mythic journey. You first feel *called to adventure* when you decide that your health is ready for a change, but there might also be the *refusal of the call*. This is when you might say to yourself that nothing has ever worked before so this isn't going to work either. However, you muster the courage and decide that you are indeed ready to step out of life as usual. This is a good time to *call upon spiritual assistance*. You then encounter the *first threshold*, in which you begin to walk away from your comfort zone. Next comes the *road of trails*, an uncomfortable, arduous quest (sometimes at this stage, it feels like nothing will ever change, and you might yearn to return to your old way of being). As you continue forward, there's a kind of *death*, or release, that occurs as you surrender to the new path. Finally, there is the *resurrection* and return back across the threshold to integrate what you've gained into your life. Stepping out of your comfort zone is truly an act of power.

Level 3: The Law of Reversal

The *law of reversal* applies to weight loss, but it can also apply to any area of your health that you want to improve. When the numbers on the scale start coming down, and you begin to lose the unneeded weight on your body, a curious phenomenon occurs. It's not uncommon for the *same kind of emotions and issues* that were occurring for you at a particular weight to arise again when you hit that weight.

For example, Caroline started this program when she was almost 200 pounds. As she began to drop the weight, she tracked the emotions she was experiencing. When she reached 184, she began to feel unaccountably sad and depressed. She checked through her old journals and realized that the last time she weighed 184 pounds was also when her brother died in an auto accident. It was during this time that Caroline was very upset because of his death.

When Caroline hit a plateau at 172, she experienced ongoing anger that fluctuated from low-grade irritation to bubbling rage. When she tracked what was occurring in her life at that weight, she realized that she had been having trouble at work that eventually culminated in her being fired. Then when she hit 165 pounds, Caroline entered into a constant state of worry; once again she was able to track it and realized that the last time she weighed that amount, she was worrying about her daughter, who had a health condition that

doctors couldn't seem to diagnose.

There's a sort of behavioral conditioned response that occurs at each plateau you reach as you drop weight. It's not uncommon for the emotions that weren't fully expressed (or that were suppressed) to be held in your body. So as the weight is released, those pent-up emotions are released as well.

This can also occur in other areas of your health. As you begin to heal, for instance, the issues that were evident at the onset of the condition have a tendency to arise—*they're coming to the surface to be released.* Be conscious of the law of reversal, and write down anything that seems appropriate in your Process Journal.

❦ ❦ ❦

Day 17

Hi!

I had a long talk with a friend today that deepened my appreciation of my body. My friend has been paralyzed from the waist down (and has the use of just one arm) since she was a teenager. A couple of months ago, she was watching a television show on yoga and decided to try to stretch her leg into a yoga position. Suddenly she heard a loud snap—she had broken her femur bone, which was weak from lack of use. (She lives alone, so this was serious.) After undergoing life-threatening surgery, she got a staph infection from the hospital, and these days, she can only sit up for maybe an hour a day. She used to be able to maneuver herself around in her electric wheelchair, but now she has lost (maybe forever) her ability to be mobile on her own.

Yet as we were talking, she didn't mention how horrific it was to lose even more physical independence. She spoke about her body as if it was a very loyal and patient friend, and she told me how much deep appreciation she felt for it. I was humbled and inspired by her. She also talked about how really excited she was to receive our old hot tub (as a gift), as the only time in her life— since her accident—that she has felt free is when she's able to float in water. (It's been seven years since she has done this.)

Right now, I'm so grateful to my friend for helping me put things in perspective. In this moment, honestly, I don't give a damn about a few extra pounds or being sedentary. I'm just so happy to be able to do mundane things like walking down the road to pick up the mail. I feel overwhelming gratitude for this loyal, wonderful body of mine. We are all so fortunate to have the bodies we have.

With a depth of love and gratitude,
Denise

Day 17 (Fire): Facing the Shadow

Many of us have parts of our bodies that we don't want to acknowledge or take responsibility for. As I have said many times, the soul loves the truth, so it's immensely important to be honest about these limiting thoughts. Also, if we wish to see the nature of our shadows, we need to be aware of our criticisms regarding the bodies of others. Often what we judge in others says something about how we view ourselves.

If you *observe* something, it's not a projection, but if you *judge* it, it is. What you pass judgment on can be a reflection of the qualities that you possess but deny within yourself.

Today is aimed at beginning—even more so—to own all of the parts of yourself in order to take responsibility for the choices you've made in life that have affected your body. This will help you become whole as you accept and honor your body (no matter what shape it's in).

Affirmation for the Day

I unconditionally accept all parts of myself.

Today

Be aware of every time you negatively judge someone because of his or her body. When you do so, ask yourself, *Could this trait possibly be something that I've exhibited in the past, am currently exhibiting, or am capable of manifesting in the future?* Just by examining your judgments, you allow integration to occur.

Reward

My reward for completing Day 17 is:

(Gift yourself this reward at the successful completion of today's exercises.)

Overview

- *Committed to Change!*
  Level 1: Your Body as a Barometer of Truth

- *Going for It!*
  Level 2: What Secret Is Your Body Harboring?

- *Playing Full Out!*
  Level 3: Explore Your Sexual History, and Dance Your Future!

Level 1: Your Body as a Barometer of Truth

You can often tell what issues you have and what beliefs you hold just by discovering what's out of whack in your body. Every gland, organ, and cell has something to say about who you are. Today, pay attention to what your body is trying to tell you. In no small way, your body is your oracle, so be open to what its signs or messages are in every moment. Your body is always telling you the truth about your life, and it knows what's genuine or significant about every situation and person you encounter. Listen, close your eyes, and ask your body what it wants to tell you.

Additionally, go through each part of your body, asking, *What is true?* For example, you might ask your ears this, and they might respond that they don't want to hear your husband when he talks about work. You might ask your shoulders what's true, and they may say that they're tired of carrying too much responsibility.

Level 2: What Secret Is Your Body Harboring?

Each of our lives is determined by our past, especially the past that is forgotten, suppressed, or denied. Do you have any secrets about your body? Is there anything about your body that you don't want anyone to know? Is there something you've done with your body that you feel ashamed of and have never told anyone? Is there something that someone has done with your body that makes you ashamed? The answer to all of these questions might be no, but if there is a *yes*, write it down. Look at it, and then ask: "So what now?" or "How is this a problem?" As you do so, notice which memories, thoughts, and energy shifts occur within you. By objectively examining your secrets, you can begin to diminish some of the effects they have on you.

If you're really "going for it!" then I suggest that you take a risk and share your secret with someone you trust. Alternatively, you might consider creating a fire ceremony and burning the secret you've written down, with the intent that the residual energy is leaving your body.

Level 3: Explore Your Sexual History, and Dance Your Future!

One of the most immediate ways to experience your body is through sexual activity. Here are your assignments: First, record your sexual history in your Process Journal. Describe your first sexual awakenings, and write about everything—the good times, the bad times, early childhood recollections . . . *from your body's point of view.* Imagine that your body is writing this, and notice what emotions and memories surface. Remember that even though you have a sexual past, you are not your past. Doing this exercise can be very liberating.

The next assignment is to take at least 30 minutes to "dance your future." What kind of body do you desire in the future? What kind of health do you wish for? What do you want your body to say about you to the world? Dance *as if* the future was here, and you're in the body you desire. *Be* the health that you dream of. If you get exhausted, dance through it, imagining that your movement radiates into the future. Write down any feelings and realizations you experience in your Process Journal.

‡ ‡ ‡

Day 18

Hi!

*Today I've been thinking about how our bodies get out of
shape in the first place. Of course, there are lots of reasons for health
concerns such as genetics, nutrition, injuries, pollution, and so on.
But many of our challenges regarding our mental and physical
well-being may have their origins from something that occurred
or something that was said in our youth. As children, our minds
are like fertile soil, and often the things we're told (or the decisions
that we make about ourselves) are the seeds that get planted in our
subconscious . . . and then bear fruit when we become adults. The
child might have consciously forgotten a parent's words, and she
doesn't realize that a negative belief is growing deep inside her, but
her subconscious will tend to the seed that has been planted and
will eventually manifest symptoms in her body.*

*There's no benefit in judging yourself for the coping modali-
ties you developed in your youth. However, until you heal the
child you were, you won't become the adult you wish to be. You
have the opportunity to begin to get to the root of any negative
beliefs that have been planted and clear them out of your soul.
The holiest ground is the soil that once grew resentment and self-
doubt; but is now producing sprouts of hope, self-esteem, forgiveness, and love.*

*Today, hold the intent that you're moving toward self-
awareness, acknowledging the stories you tell yourself that justify
the state of your health . . . and deleting those personal myths
that don't serve you. This program isn't necessarily about "getting
better"—it's about letting go of old beliefs so that your soul can
shine forth and your body can be fabulous, gorgeous, and radiant.*

With immense love,

Denise

Day 18 (Fire): Being Present and Practicing Forgiveness

The past is gone and the future is still to come. In truth, the only thing we have is the present, yet we spend so much time living in the past or thinking about the future that we don't experience the precious beauty of each moment. And as a result, we don't hear the messages that our bodies—and our cells—are trying to convey.

Every cell in your body has consciousness. Even though they didn't have microscopes, mystics from times past knew about cells and spoke of the consciousness within each cell. They understood what modern scientists know now—that each cell works for the good of the whole (your body) and maintains communication with all of the other cells. In fact, there is a constant interfacing via messenger molecules. Yet each has an independent function, and when a single cell is separated from the body (and put in a nutrient-rich solution), it transforms into a one-celled organism that retreats from stimulus and moves toward food. It has the innate consciousness to do so.

Your cells are similar to a one-celled organism. There is indeed an inherent wisdom within each that you can tune in to, but only if you're in the present moment. Today it's time to really begin to listen to the wisdom available to you from the cellular level of your body.

Affirmation for the Day

I invite the pure light of the sun into my heart.
May it shine from my heart to the world.

Today

Sit before a candle, inhale deeply, and imagine breathing in the Spirit and life force of Fire. Visualize its purifying energy surging through your entire being, consuming any impurities within you.

Reward

My reward for completing Day 18 is:

(Gift yourself this reward at the successful completion of today's exercises.)

Overview

- *Committed to Change!*
  Level 1: Release Stress—Be in the Present Moment

- *Going for It!*
  Level 2: Journey into Your Cells

- *Playing Full Out!*
  **Level 3: Embracing Forgiveness,
  and Saying Yes to Your Body!**

Level 1: Release Stress—Be in the Present Moment

The number one factor that damages your health is stress. In fact, the more stressed you are, the harder it is to heal physical conditions (and it's more difficult to lose weight). When you're under chronic stress, your pituitary gland secretes a hormone that triggers a fight-or-flight response. When this occurs, the adrenal glands respond by secreting excess cortisol. And when there is too much cortisol, your entire state of health is compromised.

Additionally, stress is the number one thing that ages your body. Of course, the stress of major life events such as losing a loved one, getting a divorce, moving, or being fired from a job can impact your health; but surprisingly, *the worst type of stress stems from prolonged unfinished tasks.* A recent study found that the ongoing anxiety of constantly putting off a chore or having a job that hangs over your head day after day (like constantly postponing changing the filter in your furnace or cleaning the garage) has the same negative impact on the body as smoking a pack of cigarettes a day! Constant low-level fear is much more debilitating than periodic high-level stress.

Ongoing stress (from unfinished tasks) is different from acute stress (like having to make time to repair a window that blew out during a storm; it eventually gets fixed).

Nagging stress is exhausting because it gnaws away at you. Moreover, it has been estimated that carrying around a lot of unfinished tasks in your life can increase your real age—*add 8 years for one persistent unfinished task, all the way to an extra 32 years for having a number of uncompleted tasks hanging over you!* So if you're 40 years old in chronological age and always feel stressed because you have a never-ending to-do list, your biological age could actually be 72! It's vital to make a plan to get those tasks done . . . or let them go!

(Incidentally, not all stress is bad. Research shows that working really hard to achieve your dreams or getting a challenging project done doesn't necessarily have a negative impact on your body. And neither do onetime stressors like losing your wallet or being in a fender bender.)

When you're *totally* in the present moment, you don't feel anxious or tense. You become stressed when you either replay the past or worry about the future. If you're constantly thinking, *Why did* [fill in the blank] *happen to me in the past?* or *I'm afraid that* [fill in the blank] *might happen in the future,* you're not fully experiencing the joy that is available in the moment.

Take time today to stay focused on the way your body feels right now. Most people miss the immediate joy that exists in every moment. If you find your mind wandering, gently say this to yourself: *I cannot change the past, and tomorrow is not here. All I need is within me right now.* And allow yourself to be fully tuned in to your body.

Level 2: Journey into Your Cells

Close your eyes and gently encourage your body to relax and your mind to become still. Ask yourself this: *If I knew what the divine consciousness in my cells had to say, what would it be?* Then write down what you become aware of in your Process Journal.

Next imagine that you're relaxing on a sunny beach . . . visualize yourself entering your body and becoming so small that you're actually voyaging into a single cell. See yourself becoming even smaller so that you can go into a DNA strand. Become even more minuscule, until you can enter the pure consciousness of that cell. As you reside in the present moment, in the divine consciousness of that cell, notice all that you're aware of. What do you see, hear, and feel? Take at least ten minutes to explore.

Level 3: Embracing Forgiveness, and Saying Yes to Your Body!

One way to begin to heal or empower the body is to embark on a journey of forgiveness. It's important to do so because we often wear our lack of forgiveness on our hips, waist, and thighs. It may also fester in our heart, lungs, liver, and throughout the entire body.

Forgiveness is freedom and can help your body freely express itself. I don't mean the "turn the other cheek" or "you were bad, but I'm a better person than you, so I forgive you" kind of forgiveness. I mean the kind in which you accept—truly accept—what others have done to you, what you have done to others, and especially what you have done to yourself. This doesn't mean that you need to forgive the act itself . . . some acts are unforgivable, but you can forgive the person for what was done. It reveals the understanding that bad behavior (yours and others) comes from either fear or ignorance, and everyone is acting out of their own early programming.

It has been said that anger is like picking up a hot coal to throw at someone, only to burn yourself; and resentment is like taking poison and hoping that the other person will die. The more you can forgive yourself and others, the healthier you will become.

One way to activate the force of forgiveness is to say *yes* to your body. Doing so creates energy that boosts your vitality. Throughout the day, choose every experience and feeling that your body has. Say yes to your eyes! Yes to your ears! Yes to your arms! Yes to your legs! Yes to your lips! Yes to your total body! Say yes to your life!

Affirm: *Yes, this is what I want right now!* Be as totally present as you can in your body. Stop every few moments just to tune in to yourself, then say to your body: *Yes! I'm here with you! I forgive and accept myself and others right now. I experience your truth in this moment . . . no matter what it is. Yes!*

Maybe you won't label all of your physical experiences as good today. That's okay, but at least be present for all of them. Allow them to be, in a spirit of acceptance and forgiveness.

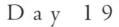

Day 19

Hi!

What an amazing experience I had today! I was outside for a few minutes, and in the far distance, I saw about 100 loudly cawing crows. I love crows and have never seen so many so close to our land. I decided to honor them by raising my arms up to the sky. In one hand, I held a piece of aluminum foil to reflect the sun so that they could see the light as my offering to them. (I know this was kind of a strange welcome, but it was all I had at the time.)

Then the most incredible thing happened: the entire flock flew directly over me. They circled right above my head, just barely 30 feet above where I stood. I felt so honored and humbled, especially since these beautiful creatures often symbolize the transition point between life and death (and that is the topic we're exploring today). I felt that it was a good sign.

All my love,

Denise

Day 19 (Fire): Facing Your Death / Embracing Your Life

Although you will never die, your body most certainly will. To the extent that you identify with your body (and not with your soul), the death process will be frightening and filled with emotional distress. If you accept death as a valuable part of your evolution as a soul, then you'll be able to fully live in the present.

Affirmation for the Day
At my source, I am divine love and light.

Today
I just saw a film in which a 60-year-old yogi went into a deep, dark hole in the ground with almost no air and no food or water for three days . . . and when she came out, she looked radiant and refreshed. In fact, she leaped over the hole with ease! It was explained that she understood that although she had a body, she didn't identify with it—she identified with God. I was impressed by this. Today, accept that you have a body, but know that when you body dies, *you* will continue.

Reward
My reward for completing Day 19 is:

(Gift yourself this reward at the successful completion of today's exercises.)

Overview

- *Committed to Change!*
  **Level 1: The Body Is the Gateway
  to the Soul**

- *Going for It!*
  Level 2: Rocking-Chair Test

- *Playing Full Out!*
  Level 3: Death as a Rite of Passage

Level 1: The Body Is the Gateway to the Soul

Even if you're given a diagnosis, you don't have to accept the prognosis. No matter what others tell you about your condition, you *don't* need to accept it unless it feels right to you.

More than 35 years ago, a doctor from China told me something that changed my life. I visited Dr. Wu because I was concerned about my tailbone, which was actually dangling by the nerve. (It had been so damaged during an accident that it wasn't connected to the rest of my spine.) Another physician had warned me that if I fell or moved in the wrong way, it could paralyze me. Dr. Wu had a great reputation, so I decided to see him for a second opinion.

After I explained the challenge and shared my fear of becoming paralyzed, he asked if I had trouble walking. I said no and that it wasn't a problem. Then he asked if I was healthy and whether or not I could run. I replied, "I'm healthy, and I run all the time."

Dr. Wu looked me straight in the eyes and asked, "Would you care if you didn't have a heart, as long as you were healthy and well?" This startled me, and my first response was: "Of course I need a heart!" He didn't say anything; he just looked at me with compassion. I sat there thinking, then slowly said, "Actually, as long as I'm healthy, I wouldn't care if I didn't have a heart." He then told me to focus on what was true—the fact that I *could* walk and run—and realize that a woman could be incredibly healthy, even if the medical profession declared that she wasn't. Dr. Wu reminded me that the human spirit (and soul) was amazing and could create miracles. Almost four decades later, I can still walk and run with ease.

The body is the gateway to the soul . . . and when you hang out in the realm of the soul, anything is possible. Is there a time in your life when you listened to the wisdom of your soul and overcame a challenge or experienced healing of some kind? Today, take a moment to imagine that you're traveling inside your body to reach the sanctuary of your soul. Be sure to write down what you experience while you're there in your Process Journal.

Level 2: Rocking-Chair Test

You have a limited number of days to occupy your body, and there are a limited number of things that you can do with it while you have it. Native Americans have an expression that I love: "It's a good day to die." To me, this means: *I accept my life in its totality. I'm complete right now. If I am to die today, I'm ready.* Have you done everything with your body that you desire? Are you ready for your body to die? If the answer is no, why not? Is it because you haven't completed something or have family or others to care for? If there's something you haven't done, plan to do it. Maybe you want to make a pilgrimage but have been putting it off for years. By the time you're finally ready to do it, will your body be ready?

Imagine yourself far into the future and you're sitting in a rocking chair, reviewing your life. You have a limited number of years, months, weeks, and days until your body dies . . . so how can you make the most of your remaining time? What are your priorities? What have you been putting off?

Remember that as the years pass, the ways in which you can use your body may change. Take snowboarding, for example—yes, it's true that you could take up snowboarding in your 60s (some people do), but that would be a dangerous activity for most people at that age. So the main point is that if there's something you've always wanted to do, don't wait until it's too late or too dangerous. *Do it now.*

Level 3: Death as a Rite of Passage

This program has been focused on the body, and the truth is that there will be a time in your evolution when you no longer possess it. There's value in being prepared for that day. Many ancient cultures included this practice in their spiritual training, as it can be a powerful rite of passage. When you face your death, you also face (and embrace) your life. You have a body. But you are *not* your body. You are eternal.

To overcome your fear of death and even accept it, it's valuable to practice dying. Of course, this doesn't mean actually dying—it means that you just practice imagining that you accept your death when the day comes, *until you no longer feel afraid.* In a strange way, when you overcome your fear of death, you dramatically strengthen your body and make it less prone to dying.

One technique athletes use to improve their performance is to visualize doing a particular activity over and over again. For example, competitive downhill skiers will repeatedly visualize themselves going down a ski run, and this tends to dramatically improve their actual performance. You can use the same technique to practice dying. Every time you imagine yourself dying (at the end of your days), see yourself slipping out of your body and journeying to a place that is exquisitely beautiful and peaceful. It might be a garden or a gentle meadow, or perhaps it's where angelic beings or your loved ones are waiting for you with open arms.

The more you can accept and even embrace the fact that your body will die, the less the fear of death will subtly penetrate into your body and everyday life. The less fear of death you have, the more fully you can live in the present moment. Create your funeral plan. What music is playing? Who's there? What's being said about you? Who will miss you? Where does your body or your ashes go? What do you want to happen to all of the possessions you'll leave behind? Where do you go after your body dies? What happens next? Write down your thoughts in your Process Journal.

‡ ‡ ‡

Day 20

Hi!

Well, after all my glorious clutter-clearing the last couple of weeks, Meadow, my daughter, came home with three huge boxes of _her_ giveaways along with an old television and a carton of videos. Nature must abhor a vacuum, because I'm now the proud owner of lots more clutter! As soon as I made some space, it just filled up again. Maybe I'm kind of a "stuffoholic" because I now seem to have as much stuff as I did before my big clutter-clearing.

But my alter ego nags me about all of Meadow's belongings, saying, "It's really good stuff . . . you never know when that new blue beaded opera bag will come in handy." (Never mind that I've only been to the opera twice in my life.) "And it's not everyone who has a boxful of ladybug citronella torches!" I mean, how did I manage without these things before?!

Hey! You only have eight more days to go, so don't give up. Keep going, and do the best you can. Remember that you started this program for a reason. There was something that you were yearning for, and it's still possible to gain amazing results. If you've been thinking, "Well, I haven't really been engaging in this program, so I'm not going to do much for the rest of it," let that thought go! Things are happening even if you're not consciously aware of them. _Your entire life can transform in the next eight days, if you're willing for it to happen!_ Be willing.

So reinstate your intention—after all, _miracles can happen_ in the next eight days. You can do it. Go for it today!

All my love,

Denise

Day 20 (Fire): You Are the Force

When you remember that you're a part of all things—and that you're not limited to the confines of your body—you can have a conscious affect on your own cells, atoms, and molecules. Today's exercises will further help you remember what's true about your body's relationship to the universe.

Affirmation for the Day
My body is a part of all things.

Today
Be kind to your body today.

Reward
My reward for completing Day 20 is:

(Gift yourself this reward at the successful completion of today's exercises.)

Overview

- *Committed to Change!*
  Level 1: You *Are* the Life-Force "Field"

- *Going for It!*
  Level 2: Cherishing Your Body

- *Playing Full Out!*
  Level 3: The Universe Flows Through Your Body: Chakras, the Universe, and Beyond

*Level 1: You **Are** the Life-Force "Field"*

There's a life-force field that's within us and around us . . . and your body isn't separate from that field. Although I don't understand the mechanics of it all, I do know, in quantum physics, that the tiniest subatomic particle is everywhere in space-time. In other words, from a scientific perspective, all the subatomic particles in your body are components of all things because of the non-locality of energy particles. Of course from a spiritual perspective, ancient sages have always asserted: "You are a part of all things." In the deepest sense, you *are* the life-force field.

Today, take time to imagine and maintain awareness that your body is a part of the subtle vibrations of "the field." (Do this as a meditation.) Communicate with the consciousness within your body, and allow that consciousness to experience liberation by visualizing a merging with "the field." This provides your cells the opportunity to absorb energy and life force from the universe, which in turn, can increase your health and vitality, as well as create a feeling of peace and well-being unlike any other. This can be a very powerful—even life-changing—process.

Level 2: Cherishing Your Body

Fire Week is the time for action, so ask yourself what you could do today that would uplift the energy within your body. If your body was an honored guest in your home, what would you do that would be deeply appreciated by this special being? Would you offer her a massage? Rub her feet? Prepare the finest tea or an amazing meal? Perhaps you would brush her hair in a luxurious manner? Maybe you would anoint her bath with rare, fragrant oils.

When you take time to cherish your body, sometimes it's the people who are the closest to you who unconsciously sabotage your decision. It's during those times that you need to put your body first, rather than try to pander to the insecurities of friends or family members.

For example, have you ever been on a food regime, exercise program, or a diet, and:

- You've been afraid to tell anyone about it because you didn't want to be judged?

- You've told your friends that you already ate— or you were going to eat later—rather than tell them that you're restricting your calories?

- You've pretended to drink or eat (but secretly dumped it) rather than have others thinking that you weren't drinking as much alcohol (or eating as much food) as everyone else?

- Others have said this to you: "You're skinny already—you don't need to diet," or "If you exercise too much, you'll lose muscle mass," or "Come on, a little bit won't hurt you"?

If you've experienced any of these situations, then I suggest that you turn them into a spiritual exercise by acknowledging your truth to the naysayers in a confident, non-defensive way. Smile and be gracious. Speak from your heart with calm, centered clarity. When you do so, you step into your strength and self-esteem. You never need to hide the fact that you're cherishing and supporting your body.

Level 3: The Universe Flows Through Your Body: Chakras, the Universe, and Beyond

Sometime today, stand naked and open to "the universe." This is the universal intelligence that permeates the vast solar systems, galaxies, interstellar space, and beyond. Stand under the sun or under the stars and moon, and imagine that the universe is flowing through you. If you can do this outside, all the better.

If you don't live in a place where you can stand outdoors without clothing, then be naked in your own home or apartment (if possible, before a window open to the sky). If this isn't possible, then stand naked somewhere in your home where you feel safe, while visualizing the stars/moon/sun above you and the universe permeating deep within you. No matter where you are, imagine that you're seamlessly merging with the cosmos. Your breath is the breath of eternity. The water in your veins has been and will be again clouds, rivers, lakes, snow, and ice. The matter in your bones has been mountains, deserts, and even stardust . . . and will be again.

As you stand nude, focus on your chakras. These are the energy centers in your body that are always flowing and changing according to your thoughts, feelings, and life circumstances. When your body is healthy and well, these energy centers create an aura that is colorful, clear, and flowing (as seen by some people). When you're ill, your chakras appear dull, lackluster, and sluggish. The vibration of each one corresponds to a different part of your body and reflects and affects the energy of those specific areas.

Chakras have a tendency to hold negative memories, beliefs, and emotions that influence your health. Limiting decisions and beliefs, therefore, get "stuck" in a chakra center. Almost all health issues have corresponding negative beliefs that are stored in one or several chakras. In order to activate vibrant health, it's immensely valuable to clear them out. To do so, imagine that as you breathe in the universe (while standing nude), you're also vigorously breathing into and out of each chakra. This is an invigorating, purifying breath. Pay particular attention to the chakras that seem to correspond to issues that you're currently dealing with in your life. The following list will help you understand which chakras might be out of balance.

First Chakra

Location: Tailbone

Influences: Lower spine, tailbone, bones, sexual and reproductive organs, genitalia, rectum, large intestine, adrenals, hips, hands, legs, feet

Associated with: Physical needs, physical life force, sexuality, survival issues, ongoing financial concerns, safety issues, fight or flight, stability, structure, groundedness, physical energy, anger (overt and covert), jealousy

Color vibration: Red

Second Chakra

Location: Five fingers below the belly button

Influences: Womb, reproductive organs, bladder, urinary tract, kidney, spleen, skin, subdermis

Associated with: Emotional needs, trust, intimacy, addictions, attachment, letting go, creativity, relationship challenges

Color vibration: Orange

Third Chakra

Location: Solar plexus

Influences: Stomach, duodenum, small intestine, digestive system, pancreas, blood sugar, liver, spleen, gallbladder, mid-arms

Associated with: Personal power issues, fear, perfectionism, willpower, courage, self-control, organization, criticalness, judgment

Color vibration: Yellow

Fourth Chakra

Location: Center of chest

Influences: Heart, thymus, lungs, blood pressure, lymphatic system, immune system, breathing, upper spine, ribs, chest, circulation system, arms, hands

Associated with: Relationship issues, love, giving and receiving, balance, flexibility, stagnation, flow, healing

Color vibration: Green

Fifth Chakra

Location: Throat

Influences: Thyroid, parathyroid, neck, shoulders, larynx, atlas, ears, nose, arms, and hands

Associated with: Communication issues, clarity, focus, speaking up, intention

Color vibration: Blue

Sixth Chakra

Location: Between and slightly above the eyebrows

Influences: Pituitary, hypothalamus, eyes, autonomic nervous system, brain

Associated with: Intuition issues, too open or closed, clairvoyance, overview, psychic awareness, taking on the issues of others, service for the good of all

Color vibration: Purple/Indigo

Seventh Chakra

Location: Top of the head

Influences: Top of the head, pineal gland, central nervous system

Associated with: Connection to Creator, spiritual love, compassion, unity with all of life, harmony, nonattachment

Color vibration: Violet

Eighth Chakra

Although not typically included in the chakra system, there is an eighth energy center. (You can feel it when someone passes their hand over your head.) This chakra is similar to the seventh one, although its focus is more on connecting with the world around you instead of something inside your body.

Location: Six inches above the head and surrounding the body

Influences: Connection with the world around you

Associated with: Connection to Creator, spiritual love, compassion, unity with all of life, harmony, nonattachment

Color vibration: White

Chakra Guardian Exercise

Relax, and close your eyes. Imagine that you're becoming very small and journeying inside your body. As you enter through the sacred gateway into each chakra center, notice the color and how bright or dim it is. Pay attention to any sounds, emotions, or memories that spontaneously appear. Then imagine that you're visiting the "Guardian" of each chakra. Usually these beings will appear in the form of a human; but sometimes you'll view them as a mythical creature, elf, fairy, angel, animal, light, or symbol. Accept whatever form the Guardian appears as. Take time to ask each Guardian if there is any information that you need to know. Write down your discoveries in your Process Journal.

✡ ✡ ✡

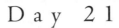

Day 21

Hi!
It's the last day of Fire! Fire has the ability to purify all that it comes in contact with. It also can ignite the glowing embers in your soul so that it becomes a vibrant flame of purity and clarity. The spiritual seeds planted in the wellspring of your being during Fire Week will continue to blossom in the months ahead. However, you may be looking forward to experiencing less emotional intensity as you move into Earth Week tomorrow.

Earth Week should help ground some of the emotions that may have been flowing so freely in the last couple weeks. However, we're still in Fire . . . so let's step into the holy flame!

I think you'll like today—its focus is on creativity and flow!
All my love . . . always and forever,
Denise

Day 21 (Fire): Fanning the Flame of Your Body's Creativity

For your body to be filled with light-force energy, it needs to express itself creatively. Creativity is one of the easiest ways to activate physical vitality and health. I knew an elderly pianist who had debilitating arthritis and endured severe pain, yet when she was playing the piano, all of her discomfort receded, and she experienced tremendous fluidity in her joints. This isn't uncommon! When inspiration is flowing, the body responds with vivacious vitality.

To fan the flames of your own creativity, allow your body to express itself in any manner it chooses while you're engaging in the exercise for today, even if it seems wild or weird. And for heaven's sake, don't judge your body. Nothing dampens creativity faster than thoughts such as *This isn't very good.* If you entertain doubts or harsh criticism about the way in which your body expresses itself, your negativity will put out your fire.

When you're being truly creative, time stands still, and you enter a dimension that can carry you beyond the ordinariness of everyday life. Ancient mystics knew this, which is why they often used creative movements to achieve a spiritual trance state.

Affirmation for the Day

Incredible, creative life force flows through my entire being.

Today

Find a different and creative way to express yourself through your body.

Reward
My reward for completing Day 21 is:

(Gift yourself this reward at the successful completion of today's exercises.)

Overview

- *Committed to Change!*
  Level 1: Listen with Your Body

- *Going for It!*
  Level 2: Boundless Body Creativity

- *Playing Full Out!*
  Level 3: Trance Dance!

Level 1: Listen with Your Body

Put some music on, close your eyes, and listen with your entire body—not just with your ears. For this Level 1 exercise, don't move or dance, just be still and absorb the energy and vibration of the music. You might want to experiment with a variety of music. Notice how different places in your body respond to particular songs or musical genres. Your body is absorbing the vibration that it needs in the places that need it.

Level 2: Boundless Body Creativity

When you allow the spirit of creativity to flow through your body, you become more fluid, flexible, supple, and vital. Physical creativity enlivens your health and helps prevent aging. For today's exercise, put some music on, close your eyes, and then focus on different parts of your body. Start by traveling into your head and neck, and ask: "How would you like to move?" or "What would you like to do now?" If you get the feeling that your head and neck just want to roll from side to side, allow that to occur.

Then, in your imagination, travel into your shoulders, and ask, "How would you like to move?" Allow your shoulders to move in any way they wish. Continue to go into every area of your body, and permit each part to move in whatever manner it desires. Remember that it doesn't have to look good or be fluid . . . it's just about your body expressing itself. When you're finished, allow *all* of the parts of yourself to freely move together. In other words, let your entire body express itself creatively, honestly, and in present time. Dance your prayers. Dance your soul.

Then stop all movement, be still, close your eyes, and ask what message your soul has for you.

Level 3: Trance Dance!

Take some time to think about all of your sub-personalities. For example, one part of you might be a Mother, another part a Lover, and other parts could be Healer, Hot and Sexy Motorcycle Mama, Warrior, and Always Afraid. All of these are important! Now draw a circle on a large piece of paper, and make a rudimentary drawing of these "parts" of yourself. You can even give them names. Notice how you've sketched each of these bodies. Are some larger and some smaller? Are any colors associated with these different "selves"? You might even want to put a percentage next to each part. For example, maybe you're Maria Mother approximately 27 percent of the time, Holly Healer 13 percent of the time, 5 percent Sassy Sue, and 55 percent Fearful Frieda.

If you repress or reject any aspects of yourself, you have less life force available to you. (You deplete your energy when you hold back or deny a part of yourself.) But if you embrace *all* of your parts, you can access incredible vitality! One way to do so is to allow each "personality" to express itself physically. For example, put some music on, close your eyes, and imagine that you're Holly Healer and move and dance as she would. Then switch into another part, and dance or move as that sub-personality until you dissolve into that part of yourself.

Once you've danced all of your "parts," now imagine that they're merged within you. Put on some drum music or any song with a good beat, and let it all go! Engage in this "trance dance" until you sense a kind of dissolving—that is, there are no sub-personalities, no floor, no ceiling, no room, no body . . . just the beat. Become the beat. Allow all emotions and images to emerge and flow through you.

Reward

My reward for completing Fire Week is:

(Gift yourself this reward at the successful completion of today's exercises.)

Your Accomplishments

Fire Week has come to a close. Take a few moments to breathe deeply and reflect on what you've accomplished during the past seven days before shifting your attention to Earth Week. Write down your achievements in your Process Journal, and be sure to reward yourself for completing Fire Week! Congratulations!

>———✢———‹

CHAPTER FOUR

Earth Week— Clearing Your Physical Body

As a child, one of my greatest joys was digging in the earth. At the base of an old oak tree, I dug a large hole that was about two feet deep and three feet wide. It was my secret dirt hole. Whenever I was upset, I ran across the grassy hills to my hole and curled up inside of it. It felt like a womb—safe and secure. I loved the smell and the texture of the loamy soil. Now as an adult, I don't curl up in "dirt holes," but whenever I need to feel grounded and connected to what's truly important in life, I call upon the spirit of

Mother Earth. Or I walk outside barefoot and feel the earth's energy flowing up through me. Connecting with the Spirit of Earth can bring you back to what is real and authentic in life.

The Next Seven Days

1. Focus on the Earth

For the week ahead, spend time focusing on the earth. When you're outside, for instance, pay attention to the ground beneath you. Even if you're walking on sidewalk, take a moment to connect with the soil beneath the concrete.

2. Nourishment from the Earth

Be aware of the foods you eat that grow from the earth, especially root vegetables.

3. Your Body's Connection to Mother Earth

Focus upon the intimate connection that your body has to Mother Earth and the fact that when you leave your physical self, it will once again return to the earth.

During Earth Week

- Detoxify your body.

- Talk to your body.

- Be conscious of the food you eat.

- Stay grounded.

- Notice how the physical energy of your home affects your health.

- Take action for your well-being in the future.

✤ ✤ ✤

Day 22

Hi!

We're in the final stretch! Today is the first day of Earth Week, and this is the time for grounding all of the "stuff" that has come up during the last three weeks. It's also the time to focus even more upon what strengthens your body.

I recently heard that you aren't truly on a spiritual path unless you're willing to anger, hurt, or disappoint people. Unless you're willing to do those things—when necessary—you are inauthentic. This was very difficult for me to hear, as I try so hard <u>not</u> to anger, hurt, or disappoint anyone. (I know this is considered dysfunctional, but it's also the truth for me.) But then I thought of my two heroes: the late Mother Teresa and the Dalai Lama. In their lives, they have both made many people angry and upset. They haven't done so to be unkind or to hurt or anger people; they've just remained authentic to their values . . . and some people haven't liked it.

When you're always tiptoeing around others, it can have a devastating effect on your health. I met a well-respected cancer doctor who told me that he had the "nicest patients." He remarked that research showed that "people pleasers" were more likely to get cancer and die from it than those who stood up for themselves.

Anyway, this is the week to batten down the hatches and really focus on expanding the consciousness within your body. Let today be a new beginning.

All my love,

Denise

Day 22 (Earth): Connecting with Your Body

Your physical body is your tool for experiencing the world. It allows you to see, hear, feel, taste, smell, touch, and know your inner and outer environments. It's also the temple for your soul. Your soul is constantly communicating with you through your body, but you're often too busy to really hear these messages. So today begins a journey to hear the messages of your body and soul.

Affirmation for the Day
I am one with the earth. I am one with my body.

Today
Do a meditation in which you imagine that you *are* planet Earth. Alternatively, imagine that you've transformed into an aspect of the earth, such as an old oak tree with your roots sinking deep into the ground or a wildflower swaying in a warm spring breeze. Your body is a part of the vast interconnected universe; this meditation helps you reconnect with the physical unity of all things.

Reward

My reward for completing Day 22 is:

(Gift yourself this reward at the successful
completion of today's exercises.)

Overview

- *Committed to Change!*
  Level 1: How Do You Define Your Body?

- *Going for It!*
  **Level 2: How Does Your Body Affect
  Your Identity?**

- *Playing Full Out!*
  **Level 3: What Am I Pretending
  Not to Know?**

Level 1: How Do You Define Your Body?

The way you relate to your body is often based on
what you compare your body to. For example, compared to a mouse, you're really big, but compared to an
elephant, you're quite small. The conclusions you form
actually depend upon what you judge yourself against.
You know that you're a female because you see males,
and you know that you're not one of those. You know

that you're short because you see tall people . . . and you know that you're not one of those. You know that you're old because you see younger people (and you know that you're no longer one of those).

Perhaps you compare yourself to yourself. Do you say, "I *used* to be 20 pounds lighter"? Do you compare yourself to your teenage self, saying, "I *used* to be able to stay up late and not be tired the next morning"? Maybe you compare your present body with the one you had when you got married: "I *used* to fit in a size-10 dress." Most people define themselves by the body they occupy, and then they define their body by contrasting it to their surroundings.

However, try this instead: Imagine that you're floating in space. All memory of your past is gone. All recollections of the comparisons you've made in your life are gone. You are just a naked body drifting in the vastness of space. When there's nothing to compare your body to, how do you define it? It's not skinny or fat, tall or short, or young or old. All of your perceptions are a delusion—they have nothing to do with who you are. The only thing that you have is your senses . . . and the present moment. In other words, what are you seeing, sensing, smelling, feeling, and touching right now? This is the truth about your body. (It's very difficult to define your body without comparing it to something or someone else. Be sure to choose comparisons that make you feel good about yourself and your body, rather than ones that damage your self-esteem.)

Level 2: How Does Your Body Affect Your Identity?

How you carry your body affects your identity. If you hold your body in a rigid manner, it wouldn't be uncommon to have an identity of a rigid person. If you hold your body in a slovenly way, it wouldn't be strange to have the identity of a careless person. Most people tend to get stuck with one identity and one usual way of positioning their bodies. Today's exercise is focused on changing your identity through changing the way in which you use your body.

Stand in front of a tall mirror. If possible, stand naked. Then begin to make faces—any kind of face, such as funny, silly, mad, peaceful, and so on. Find creative ways to do so, and allow your body to follow suit. Discover new ways to use your face and body together. Notice how you now feel about yourself and your body based on the different ways you use your body. Be sure to write about your experience in your Process Journal.

Level 3: What Am I Pretending Not to Know?

Simply sit or lie down in a relaxed and loose position. Breathe. Wait. Know that the Creator exists in your body. Close your eyes and slowly go through each part of your body, starting with your feet. Give each part of yourself a personality, and imagine speaking to that part to see if there is anything that it wants you to know. Ask yourself: *If there was something regarding this part of my body that*

I'm pretending not to know, what would it be?

Also ask yourself what triggers you to do the things that damage your health. For example, I often overeat when I'm tired or bored. Some people drink too much when they're sad. List the events, feelings, or emotions that trigger bad habits. What are some ways you can address those triggers without damaging your health?

Complete the meditation by telling each part how much you love and appreciate it. When you're finished, if you learned anything that requires you to take action, make a plan to do so.

D a y 2 3

Hi!

    I've been thinking about the power of our thoughts on our health and came across some interesting research. Numerous studies support the idea that people with a positive outlook tend to be much healthier and enjoy longer lives than those who are pessimistic about the future. In a long-term California study, people who expected the worst in life had a 25 percent higher risk of dying before age 65.

    In another study, researchers rated 1,000 Dutch men and women—ages 65 to 85—regarding their degree of optimism about the future. After ten years, the participants who were classified as being optimistic had <u>55 percent fewer deaths</u> than the pessimists. Additionally, Harvard researchers found that a negative outlook had an effect on heart disease. Starting in 1988, they studied 1,306 men who had been rated for optimism and pessimism. During the following ten years, the men who reported strong levels of optimism had <u>almost half</u> the risk of suffering heart disease than the naysayers. Similar statistics were found in a study of 600 people—over age 50—in a small Ohio town in 1975. Researchers found that the optimists lived about 7.5 years longer than participants with a more dismal perspective.

    All of this research, plus volumes more, gives credence to the belief that your attitude about the future can influence your health.

    Hey, there's only a few more days to go . . . make the most of them!

    All my love,

    Denise

Day 23 (Earth): Body Detox

There is a powerful correlation between your body and your life—if your body is sluggish and stagnant, it's easier to feel that way yourself. When your body is vibrant and singing with life-force energy, your spirit soars.

Modern life is often toxic to the soul. In addition to the stress of constantly hurrying and being busy, we also don't always take time to eat in a leisurely way—instead, we grab fast food, wolf it down (barely tasting it), and run off to the next thing. Much of our water and air is polluted, and much of our food has been produced using pesticides and chemicals. To maintain a healthy environment for the soul, it's valuable to periodically detoxify our body.

Affirmation for the Day

*My mind, body, and spirit are
clear channels for Spirit.*

Today

Breathe deeply, stretch, and drink lots of water. Eat lightly and consume fresh food that has life force in it. Walk, dance, and move your body.

Reward
My reward for completing Day 23 is:

(Gift yourself this reward at the successful completion of today's exercises.)

Overview

- *Committed to Change!*
  Level 1: Detoxing Pessimism

- *Going for It!*
  Level 2: Cleanse or Clog, Heal or Steal

- *Playing Full Out!*
  **Level 3: The Ultimate Detox:
  What Traps You? What Frees You?**

Level 1: Detoxing Pessimism

When you think about your future, do you feel excited and positive, or do you worry and have concerns? Are you apprehensive that something bad will happen? Do you think there won't be enough money (or love, food, shelter, and so on) down the road? Are you worried about your health several years from now? Are you troubled about Lyme disease, West Nile virus, pollution, breast cancer, heart disease, pandemic flu, terrorist attacks, nuclear fallout, AIDS, or some other event or disaster?

The media capitalizes on this kind of anxiety. In fact, when you listen to television reports, your fears may seem totally justified, so it's easy to be pessimistic. *Paradoxically, the more fearful you are about your health in the future, the more likely you are to be unhealthy.* Always being afraid can put you into a constant state of stress, anxiety, and apprehension . . . and this in turn can motivate over-eating, have a diminishing effect on your immune system, and raise your stress hormones to damaging levels.

To release pessimism, write down a list of every scary thought you have about the future. Then question each one by asking yourself: *Is this really something that I should be frightened about?* If it is, make a plan to take action, but if it isn't, let it go. The more you can look to the future with a feeling of bright, shining optimism, the more likely you are to be vibrant and healthy in the years ahead. *Being an optimist is a choice.* It's not something that you're necessarily born with or that just happens. You can choose to be positive. See your world in the best possible way, and you will be healthier and more vital.

Level 2: Cleanse or Clog, Heal or Steal

You know which foods your body needs or doesn't need. If you were to have blood work done, you could see that your cells know which foods create inflammation and which ones provide nourishment. However, this knowledge also dwells within you. By being still and tuning in, you can sense which foods are going to cleanse, heal, and strengthen your body and which are going to clog it and steal necessary nutrients. For the rest of the week, be aware of the food you're eating.

Today, with everything you eat, ask yourself, *Does this cleanse or clog me?* If a predominance of your food choices are clogging and stealing, then consider making a commitment for the rest of this program to only consume what heals and cleanses your body.

There isn't one diet that's right for everyone because we're all unique; however, there's a place within *you* that knows which foods support your body and which damage it. Relax, breathe, and close your eyes. Ask your higher self what the most empowering foods for *your* body are, and then commit to eating those foods for the next six days.

Level 3: The Ultimate Detox: What Traps You? What Frees You?

There are many ways to detoxify the body. You can eat lighter fare, for example, by consuming lots of raw organic vegetables and salads. You can drink detoxifying herbal teas or "green" drinks. Or you can also increase the amount of water you drink, or simply drink your water with a squeeze of fresh lemon. You can cleanse yourself by practicing rapid breathing, alternating with deep, full breathing; or sign up for a colonic to cleanse your bowels. As valuable as all of this can be (and it's all suggested for you on this 28-day program), even more powerful for your health is the detoxifying and releasing of negative addictive behaviors. One of the ways to do so is to focus on the people and situations that give you joy and make you feel free and expansive.

After the Vietnam War, Canadian psychologist Bruce Alexander (from Simon Fraser University) embarked on a study to understand why veterans—who had been addicted to drugs in Southeast Asia—were able to stop using them fairly easily once they returned home. Through extensive research, Alexander began to compare human addiction with induced addiction in rats. Armed with the realization that a rat's nervous system is like a human's in many ways (rats don't like to be caged any more than people do), he proceeded with his experiment.

He divided a group of rats into two living spaces: One group moved into a wonderful living space called "Rat Park." This sanctuary had tunnels and great places to burrow and roam. He put the other group in typical laboratory cages. He then offered both groups morphine-laced water and regular water. The caged rats immediately slurped up the morphine water, but remarkably, the park rats only drank the plain water.

Then Alexander took the experiment a step further: he added sugar to the morphine water to make it even more enticing for the park rats. And although rats generally love sugar water, the park rats *still* preferred the plain water. He then took the hapless caged rats (which were hardcore addicts by this point, after consuming morphine for 57 days), and moved them into Rat Park, where he allowed them to choose between the morphine solution and plain water. Amazingly, the drug-addicted rats drank the plain water. Even though they had to go through the pain of withdrawal, they still weaned themselves to the plain water. Alexander realized that *when the rats felt happy, they were drawn to that which empowered their health. When they were unhappy and felt trapped and confined, they were drawn into addictive behaviors.*

This study has a profound message for us. When we feel trapped, caged, powerless, suffocated, overwhelmed, hopeless, worthless, or resentful, we're more likely to be drawn to behaviors that damage our health. We are more likely to overeat, not exercise, drink too much, and generally do things that are destructive to our well-being. However, when we feel free, expansive, and joyous, we are less likely to be drawn to these negative behaviors.

Addictions can take many forms, including anything you do in a repetitive and obsessive way that damages your body or your life. For serious addictions to alcohol, drugs, gambling, taking dangerous risks, or shoplifting, get professional help. It's difficult (and often even impossible) to stop on your own. But there are many addictive behaviors that you can conquer on your own, such as repetitively judging yourself, constantly bowing to the criticism of others, putting the needs of others above your own, maintaining the "disease to please" to the detriment of your health and well-being, or habitually overeating without tasting your food. The first step is awareness and then being willing to take action to move forward in your life.

You are a powerful spiritual being even if you aren't consciously aware of it. You have the ability to release some of the addictive behaviors that might be damaging your body.

Think about the following questions, and write down your responses in your Process Journal:

1. Do you have any addictive behaviors or habits that damage your health (such as overeating, overdrinking, mindlessly inhaling junk food, engaging in self-destructive acts, or spending massive amounts of time in front of the TV or computer)? Make a list.

2. What and/or who in your life traps you? Make a list and notice any commonalities.

3. What and/or who in your life frees you? Make a list and notice any commonalities.

4. How can you increase the things in your life that free you? Make a list and take action on at least one item.

Day 24

Hi!

Today we're having torrential rains. Because of this, big boulders are rolling down the sides of cliffs onto the canyon road to my house. There are also places where there are mini-landslides.

As I was swerving around boulders on the road today, I thought, "Well, it makes sense. It _is_ Earth Week!"

I believe in the synchronicities that occur in life, so I began looking at the "boulders" of limiting beliefs that I have about my body. In fact, I had a bit of a breakthrough as I maneuvered through some of this rocky terrain. But today's exercises helped me stay grounded while I did so.

Only five more days to go!

All my love . . . always and forever,

Denise

Day 24 (Earth): Staying Grounded

It's not an accident that we use the word _grounded_ to indicate that we're feeling stable and centered. In no small way, the energy of the earth beneath us allows us to connect with our roots and to feel secure.

Whether you take time to walk barefoot on the earth, reach your hands into Mother Earth's rich soil, or simply imagine a flow of connective energy between you and the earth, it helps you become grounded, centered, and in touch with your deeper inner truth.

Affirmation for the Day
My body is incredibly strong and healthy.

Today
Carry yourself as if an incredible life force and confidence were flowing out of every pore of your body.

Reward
My reward for completing Day 24 is:

(Gift yourself this reward at the successful completion of today's exercises.)

Overview

- *Committed to Change!*
  Level 1: What Does Your Body Tell the World?

- *Going for It!*
  Level 2: Ancestral Bequest: The Presence of Ancestors in Your Genes

- *Playing Full Out!*
  Level 3: Staying Grounded

Level 1: What Does Your Body Tell the World?

Have you noticed how much you can tell about people simply by the way they carry their body? As you grew up, you adopted beliefs about who you are and your values and rules for life . . . *and each belief has an associated physiology.* For example, those who have low self-esteem will adopt a physiology that says: "I'm not very confident." Their bodies become so used to that position that even when they're not feeling a strong lack of self-worth, their bodies remain fixed, which counteracts any positive feelings.

Remember that your body is always communicating statements about who you are to your inner self and to the world. This is great when the message is empowering, but it's not very beneficial if the message doesn't support your well-being.

If a stranger were to watch the way you use your body, what kind of judgments might that person make about you? Would he or she think that you're vibrant, tired, healthy, arrogant, loving, peaceful, submissive, stressed, confident, busy, overwhelmed, centered, frenetic, joyous, irritated, or kind?

Today, notice how you carry yourself. Are you communicating a message to the world that is positive and satisfies you? If not, what would you need to change to carry your body in a way that conveys who you truly are and what you desire to be?

Level 2: Ancestral Bequest:
The Presence of Ancestors in Your Genes

Your ancestors are literally a part of you, via their presence in your genes. Within each of your cells is a microscopic trace of every single one of your forebears. Physical resemblances, as well as psychological profiles and types of mannerisms and behaviors, will be associated with a particular family line. Part of your personality is a result of inherited ancestral patterns, even if you were adopted. Qualities are passed down from one generation to the next, even without individual family members being aware that the specific patterns and beliefs they hold aren't universal but are particular to their own lineage.

You've cleared so much body static during these last weeks that by simply going on an inner journey, you can tap into the wisdom and voices of your ancestors— the ancestral soul that dwells within you. You can also discover—and begin to release—the negative family patterns that have lodged in your cells.

Today, go on a meditative journey in order to unlock the secret messages of your ancestors that dwell in your cells. What do your ancestors want you to know? How can they help you ground yourself? If you uncover any negative patterns that have been passed down to you, create a Power Affirmation (to release this programming) and repeat it with passion throughout the day. (For more information on this subject, see my book *Four Acts of Personal Power: How to Heal Your Past and Create a Positive Future.*)

Level 3: Staying Grounded

The power of the Earth element is to help you feel grounded and centered. This in turn allows you to rest and rejuvenate. In addition to carrying your body in ways that exemplify vitality, confidence, or vibrant health, it's also immensely valuable to use your body's physiology to typify being grounded, which will allow you to relax and feel renewed.

It's important to stay grounded, especially if we've been feeling scattered and pulled in every direction. Most of us forget how necessary it is to take time throughout the day to renew and recover our life force. We often give out so much energy that it's difficult to completely recoup it during the night, so we're often in an energy-deficient state without a reserve to call upon.

To build an enormous reserve of vital energy, it's essential to periodically take time to rejuvenate yourself, and you can use your physiology to do so. Here's an exercise to help you achieve this:

1. Begin with a few deep breaths.

2. Stand tall and imagine that there are roots growing out of the bottom of your feet, connecting you to the center of the earth.

3. Visualize yourself pulling all the stability of the earth into your body.

4. Imagine that branches are growing out of you
    and into the sky, drawing light and oxygen
    into every cell of your body.

5. Feel deeply relaxed, grounded, and sustained
    by the earth below and the heavens above.

By simply using your physiology, you can rejuvenate yourself. Think about it: When you're truly relaxed, how do you hold your body? Are your shoulders comfortable? Is your breath slow and deep? Are the muscles in your face slack? Are you softly smiling? Today, every couple of hours, take seven to ten minutes to recharge by changing your physiology into a state of peace, serenity, softness, receptivity, and joy. By doing so, you will begin to develop a bountiful, grounded reserve of life force.

Day 25

Hi!

Love must be in the air. The birds are singing so sweetly, and our chickens are laying eggs in abundance. Bogart, our baby rooster, sounds like he's getting ready to crow—he's making kind of weird gurgling sounds and seems really proud of himself. My heart is filled with gratitude.

When you embarked on this journey to empower your body, you may have noticed that not only was your body changing, but the way you interacted with others also began to change. (There is a deep connection between the way you relate with others and the health of your body.)

There's a common experience that usually begins to occur at this point in the program, especially if—in the past—you put everyone else's needs before your own. You may notice that you're beginning to take care of yourself first. However, what often happens is that those who always counted on you to be the caretaker or to put aside your needs for theirs get cranky with you. They expect you to stay as you were, and they'll do whatever they can to reel you back into the old you. Please don't fall back into the "disease to please." This doesn't support your spiritual growth or the health of your body. Those who are only your friends as long as you're pleasing them and taking care of them first are not true friends.

Today's exercises are some of the most powerful in the entire program. I send you immense blessings!

All my love,
Denise

Day 25 (Earth): Radiating Love Through Your Cells

Your cells aren't separate from your body nor are they separate from the cadence of the universe. You live in a rhythmic universe—that is, every part of nature has a unique language and rhythm of its own. Every flower, bird, and tree (and every cell) has its own language, which together creates the underlying context that weaves all of life together. You are constantly surrounded—and a part of—these rhythms of energy. If you take a moment to become very still, you can feel these rhythms *and* the consciousness of the radiant world inside each cell.

Affirmation for the Day
My cells radiate incredible life-force energy.

Today

There is love in your cells. In the vast inner space of each cell dwells infinite love. Today, take time to imagine that you're entering this sacred realm, and bask in the radiant light that exists there.

Reward

My reward for completing Day 25 is:

(Gift yourself this reward at the successful completion of today's exercises.)

Overview

- *Committed to Change!*
  Level 1: Rhythmic Breath of Love

- *Going for It!*
  Level 2: Loving Yourself, Loving Your Body

- *Playing Full Out!*
  Level 3: Putting Your Needs First

Level 1: Rhythmic Breath of Love

To invite incredible energy into your body, imagine that you're breathing love into each cell in your body as you deeply inhale. Visualize each cell humming its own song but in harmony with every other cell so that you're vibrating with a new frequency. As you surrender to this, your auric field (the energy field around you) changes and a warmth grows inside of you.

Now allow your breaths to become faster and faster . . . deeper and deeper until a rhythm develops. With each breath, see the room that you're in filling with love. If you get dizzy, slow down, but as soon as you feel better, pick up the speed a bit. Continue this for three minutes. (This is one of the most powerful exercises in this program for your health and vitality.)

Level 2: Loving Yourself, Loving Your Body

The path to radiant well-being is through love, and the most important person to love is yourself. As you're filled with loving-kindness, this also positively affects your health (and this spills over to others). Take some time today to examine if there are things in your life that you do (on a consistent basis) to please others or to meet their expectations, but that don't empower you or bring you joy. For example, do you always agree to babysit your grandkids even when there is seemingly no appreciation, and oftentimes, there's no happiness in doing so? Are you always expected to carpool to games, even when it's inconvenient for you? Know that the more you follow your own star, stop trying to please everyone, and support your own needs in life, the healthier (and happier) you will be.

Now is the time to make a stand. What can you drop from your life that doesn't bring you joy? Take action today. In the beginning, it might upset a few applecarts, but please keep going . . . do not waver! *This is the most important step you can take to empower your life and strengthen your body.* Remember, the soul (and the body) loves the truth!

Level 3: Putting Your Needs First

Take out your Process Journal, and make a list of every area in your life where you're putting the needs of others above your own. Take your time, and include everything. Then next to each item, write down what you think is the *worst* that could happen if you stopped this pattern. Would you potentially lose a friend? Would you face harsh criticism?

Then write down the *best* things that could happen if you dropped the pattern. Would you have more time for yourself? Would your self-esteem soar? Would your health improve? Ask yourself if the gains are worth the risks of dropping those self-effacing patterns. If the answer is *yes,* make a plan to drop those patterns.

‡ ‡ ‡

Day 26

Hi!

Well, there's no doubt that it's Earth Week! We had a shaker today. It was only a small earthquake, but the epicenter was close, so we really felt it. The birds became very quiet beforehand and stopped singing completely; their silence was so unusual that it caught my attention. Perhaps they were tuning in to the coming quake.

If animals are sensitive to the ebb and flow of the earth's energy, most certainly we are, too . . . but usually we just aren't as conscious of it as they are. Hopefully, all that we've done over the last month will deepen our ability to be more aware of and in harmony with the energies of the earth.

Today's assignment is about something close to my heart: creating a home for the body (and soul). The objects in your home and environment deeply affect your physical being. Here's an example: I was in Sweden and there was an abstract photo on the wall in the lodge where I was staying. One day, I thought I was coming down with a cold, but when I walked by the photo, I instantly felt better. Realizing the connection, I just stood in front of the photo, feeling better and better.

Later on when the caretaker was there, I asked him about the photograph. He informed me that it was a close-up of the molecular structure of vitamin C. I've always responded well to taking this vitamin, but I hadn't brought any with me on my trip. I never would have thought that just a photo of it could influence the way I felt, but it did. Simply standing before an image of vitamin C had a healing effect on my body.

I mention this experience as a way of introducing you to the idea that <u>everything</u> in your environment will affect your health and vitality . . . either in a positive or negative way. All things will either take your life-force energy up or down, so today's exercises are focused on becoming aware of and identifying them.

I hope you enjoy this day.

All my love,

Denise

Day 26 (Earth): A Home for Your Body

Almost all ancient and native cultures around the world practiced feng shui in one form or another. It's been around for so many centuries because it works. Your body and sense of well-being are constantly affected by the energy in your home. So if you create a feeling of vibrant health and vitality, you're much more likely to be healthy. And if the energy in your home is stagnant or dull, this will also have a profound effect on your health.

Affirmation for the Day
I am at home in my body, no matter where I am.

Today
Take some time to observe how your body feels in different environments. Just close your eyes and scan your body to notice what kind of environments takes your energy up and what kind brings it down.

Reward
My reward for completing Day 26 is:

(Gift yourself this reward at the successful completion of today's exercises.)

Overview

- *Committed to Change!*
  Level 1: Does Your Home Nurture Your Body?

- *Going for It!*
  Level 2: Your Body and Your Soul Yearn for Light

- *Playing Full Out!*
  Level 3: Creating Sacred Space for Your Body

Level 1: Does Your Home Nurture Your Body?

Walk into various rooms in your home, close your eyes, and notice how your body feels in each area. Sit and stand in various spots. Wherever you stop, close your eyes, tune in to your body, and notice what you're experiencing physically. What areas make you feel vital and filled with radiant health? Are there rooms where you start to feel sluggish and dull? Also pay attention to whether your energy rises or falls (or is neutral) in each place. Write down what you discover in your Process Journal.

Level 2: Your Body and Your Soul Yearn for Light

As you walk around your home, notice the places that make you feel clear, light, and vibrant. If there's no place that makes you feel this way, consider what you can do

to bring the feeling of light into your living spaces. This could include clutter-clearing, opening the curtains, cleaning the windows, or moving an extra lamp into the room. Also, be aware of the places where *you* feel bright. Your soul hungers for light . . . where are the places in your home that help you connect with the vast inner beauty and light within you? When you enter those realms, your soul's destiny becomes clearer, and it becomes easier to allow your spiritual source to direct your life.

Level 3: Creating Sacred Space for Your Body

Make one place in your home dedicated to your health and well-being. It might be an altar-like area that has fresh flowers or photos that feel alive with energy and life force. Creating this sacred place and keeping it clean and replenished can be a powerful metaphor for renewal and rejuvenation of your health. (You might even include a photo of yourself in it when you were feeling fabulous!) Spend ten minutes in this sacred space revitalizing yourself.

‡ ‡ ‡

Day 27

Hi!

Something wonderful happened today. Usually I'm up at 4 A.M. and have energy to last all day, but today I took a quick power nap on the couch. David said that he heard me talking in my sleep. I was saying, "I <u>love</u> my body. I <u>love</u> my body. <u>I love you,</u> body!" I think my dream was a result of my continuing to clutter-clear my photographs. As I've been sifting through them, I've been looking at the body shapes I've occupied in my life—from infant to teen to adult. I've realized that, in essence, all those bodies are dead   the cells in them are no more. The molecules in those particular bodies don't exist in me now. I'm no longer the six-year-old I once was, nor am I that 16 year old girl. She is dead, as is the infant Denise.

This might seem rather morbid, but I actually got excited when I thought about this because the truth is that although the body is dying, it's also regenerating itself, fresh and renewed in every moment. This is fascinating because it really does mean that it's possible to re-create our bodies.

I think the reason our lives seem to be continuous is because of our memories, but even those are fluid. And the remarkable thing is that we can transform our physical selves with our thoughts. Recently there was a study conducted with overweight maids who were randomly divided into two groups. One group was told that just by changing sheets and sweeping floors, they were getting a lot of exercise—in fact, even more than they needed. The other group was told nothing. Interestingly, the maids in the group who <u>believed</u> they were getting a lot of exercise began to lose weight, have lower blood pressure, and notice increased motor functions—without changing their routine—while the other group stayed the same. The premise of the researchers was that if we <u>believe</u> we're exercising, our body responds accordingly.

Anyway, I thought I'd share a few of my musings. After today, there's just one more day to go . . . remember, breakthroughs can happen in an instant. Even a minute can change your life, and you have two glorious days filled with lots and lots of minutes!

All my love,

Denise

Day 27 (Earth): Creating Fabulous Health for Your Future

You've done a substantial amount of inner and outer work to activate your health and vitality during these last weeks. However, health is a lifelong pursuit—it needs to be attended to on a daily, monthly, and yearly basis. So today, you'll begin to create strategies for your future health.

Affirmation for the Day
My body is always filled with vitality, joy, and peace!

Today

Tomorrow's future is being created today, and today is yesterday's future. So act in accordance with whom you desire to be tomorrow—in other words, your future is created now. If you wish to be strong, energetic, and physically fit, act as if you are these qualities now. Don't slouch your shoulders and drag your feet—stand tall, square your head on your shoulders, and walk with confidence and deliberation. See yourself as someone who's incredibly fit and healthy, act as if it's so . . . and so it will be. It's truly the law of attraction. As you feel it, you become it. This is a simple yet powerful truth.

Reward

My reward for completing Day 27 is:

(Gift yourself this reward at the successful completion of today's exercises.)

<u>Overview</u>

- *Committed to Change!*
  Level 1: Creating Your Healthy Future

- *Going for It!*
  Level 2: Projecting Yourself into Your Future

- *Playing Full Out!*
  Level 3: Taking Action for a Positive Future

Level 1: Visualizing Your Healthy Future

Close your eyes and spend 15 minutes visualizing an amazing, healthy future. Make it almost like an epic movie. Imagine yourself in the future doing something that someone with an incredibly vibrant body would do. Immerse yourself so much in the experience that it feels real. Write down your feelings in your Process Journal.

Level 2: Projecting Yourself into Your Future

Spend some time designing your future. In your Process Journal, write about it in detail as if you were composing from the vantage point of one year *in the future.* Use loving words and descriptions, and congratulate yourself for who you've become and all that you've experienced. For example, you might write: "The last year has been amazing! My body is stronger than it has been in years. I began to move, dance, and stretch myself physically; and it was incredible how quickly my muscles and entire body responded."

Next, try doing this exercise from the viewpoint of 3, 5, 10, 15, and even 20 years down the line. Make it feel real! By doing so, you're projecting your positive energy into the future so that it can draw to it the forces it needs to manifest.

Level 3: Taking Action for a Positive Future

You can create your future (and even dramatically change your life) simply by altering your physiology. Your emotions are a complex pattern of physiological states that are triggered by your body's movements and the way in which you hold yourself. When your brain gets messages from your body that you feel great, your health soars. And when your brain gets messages that you're stagnant, afraid, or depressed, then that's what you become. Today, choose how you want your body to feel, and then *act as if* you're feeling that way.

You might decide to feel incredible vitality. Stand in front of a mirror and arrange your facial muscles, your posture, your shoulders, and your breathing—position your entire body into the state you desire . . . even if it feels like you're faking it. Continually put yourself into that empowering physiological state during the day. Walk and move as if you were totally experiencing strength and vitality. This communicates to your subconscious in a dynamic manner that this is what's true about your health. It also sends a message to others that this is who you are, and they will reflect that back to you.

There's a direct correlation between your thoughts and emotions and your health. If you believe—and act *as if*—you're already feeling terrific, it's much easier to maintain your good health. Today's assignment may be a bit challenging, but it's well worth the rewards. From the moment you finish reading this entry, act as if your compelling, *healthy* future has already happened.

If you wish to feel sparkling vitality, for example, then act as if you already do. Walk like someone who feels sparkling and vital. Carry yourself as if you have powerful, limber muscles; and even dress as if you're incredibly healthy. Think in the same way that someone who's in terrific shape would. Every time you catch yourself slipping, snap yourself back into the positive persona of your future self.

Remember that the future is being shaped right now. So this very minute, begin to create the positive future you desire. Instead of "I'll believe it when I see it," your motto is: "I'll see it when I believe it." Start affirming that you can *and will* have an incredible future, no matter how unlikely it may seem from where you are in your current life circumstances. And so it will be!

‡ ‡ ‡

Day 28

Hi!

You did it! You made it to the last day. Congratulations!

The final day focuses on love. This is the most important ingredient of vibrant health. When you feel deeply and pro-foundly loved (and when you deeply and profoundly love yourself and others), your health soars. This is truly the secret message from your body. Enjoy your last day.

In the past four weeks, you've planted spiritual seeds in the fertile soil of your soul. These seeds will indeed take root and bear fruit of radiant well-being in the future. The results will continue long after this 28-day period. To stay on the path, make a commitment to tune in to the wisdom of your body once a day and ask what messages it has for you.

You have my immense love and support for the journey ahead. May your health become even more vibrant and sparkling!

All my love,
Denise

Day 28 (Earth): Dance Your Prayers

When you've cleared away inner and outer clutter and you've paid attention to the secret messages from your body and taken time to cherish them, your capacity to love yourself, others, and the Creator is magnified. Today is a reminder of who you are.

Affirmation for the Day

I love my body, and my body loves me. Love radiates through every cell in my body!

Today

Continually remind yourself that no matter what judgments you make about your body, you have the perfect body for the spiritual journey that you've chosen for this life.

Reward

My reward for completing Day 28 is:

(Gift yourself this reward at the successful completion of today's exercises.)

Overview

- *Committed to Change!*
  Level 1: Dance Your Prayers

- *Going for It!*
  Level 2: Open Your Heart of Light

- *Playing Full Out!*
  Level 3: Go to the Center of Your Being

Level 1: Dance Your Prayers

Stand in a very relaxed way, breathe deeply, and wait for the Creator to work within you and through you. Put yourself in a calm, peaceful state, holding the intention: *I am open to your will.*

Allow your body to be receptive to whatever experience comes. It's rather like people who do automatic writing—they hold a pen and then it seems as if some energy fills them, and their hand starts to move. Wait. Don't be startled if your body begins to shake or spontaneously do flowing motions. Your body is a receiving station for Spirit. Allow the faith and love of Spirit to flow through you. Your dance and movement is "prayer made visible." Dance your prayers. Dissolve into the prayer. Let Spirit flow through your body.

Level 2: Open Your Heart of Light

Love your body. Let your body be adored. As you praise and appreciate your splendid body—no matter what shape it's in—the healthier you will be. True love is unconditional acceptance; practice witnessing your body as it journeys through the day . . . but do this without judgment. Just observe with compassion. Try this while walking, eating, sitting, and working. When you enter a true place of witnessing, the sweet nectar of the divine has descended upon you.

Level 3: Go to the Center of Your Being

Your physical form is a reflection of your beliefs, thoughts, and decisions about yourself; but there's a deeper place inside of you that remembers who you are. It's through your physical self that you can reach the profound love of Spirit. *Your body is the sacred portal to the soul!*

To go to the center of your being, you need to let go of your rational mind, your thoughts, and your ideas. One way to do so is to shake your body! Put some rhythmic music on, wear loose clothing, breathe fully and deeply, and shake. Let your body vibrate, and lose yourself. This is a wonderful practice because it gets you out of your normal postures that define and confine you. Shake! Be wild! Dissolve yourself and your identity. If you get tired, keep going. Shake beyond the tiredness to the other side where you feel your movement as a kind of divine flow.

Then collapse (if possible onto the earth). Turn off the music, close your eyes, and softly travel to the center of your being. Enter the sacred place within you where your soul dwells. Be aware of emotions, feelings, images, and symbols that appear.

At this point, you can also ask a heartfelt question, and then simply relax and scan your entire body until you come to a spot that draws you. Move into that specific area, and ask what the message is. Almost always an insight will come forward. In addition, ask which foods, vitamins and minerals, stones, colors, oils, exercises, and affirmations you need for optimum health.

After all the clearing you've done over the last 28 days, you can finally touch this sacred, wise place inside of you. Reach out to it often in order to find the answers to your questions and hear the messages from your soul. (When you're finished, be sure to write about your experience and any insights you received in your Process Journal.)

Reward

My reward for completing Earth Week is:

(Gift yourself this reward at the successful completion of today's exercises.)

Your Accomplishments

Earth Week has come to a close. Take a few deep breaths, and reflect on what you've accomplished during the past seven days before shifting focus to the Quest. Write down your achievements and any realizations or insights in your Process Journal. Claim your gift for completing Earth week, and be sure to celebrate!

CHAPTER FIVE

Quest—Beyond the 28 Days

Y ou've spent 28 days exploring the secret messages in your body, clearing your closets, purifying yourself, and examining the deeper issues lodged within you. After all of this preparation, you're ready for the Quest. This is a time to be still . . . and just listen. Your body and your soul have their own unique language, but it's difficult to hear them unless you're quiet. Your Quest can be an hour, several hours, half a day, or even an entire day dedicated to praying and listening.

To prepare for your Quest, you might want to make a sacred circle to sit in. To do so, use objects to represent Air, Water, Fire, and Earth for the four cardinal directions. For example, you could place a feather in the eastern part of the circle to represent Air, a bowl of water in the southern area to represent Water, a candle in the west for Fire, and a crystal or stone in the north for Earth. You can make the outline of your circle out of flowers, pebbles, pinecones, or anything that's available. The objects you use are less important than the feeling you have within your circle.

Your sacred circle can be inside or outside in nature. It can be a small circle that's four to six feet wide or a larger one that's eight to ten feet wide. It's up to you; however, it's essential that while you're sitting in your circle, you feel safe. Your circle serves as your sanctuary. It becomes a hallowed point between Heaven and Earth, so it's important that you bless it when it's complete. Ask for spiritual guidance, then sit in your circle and visualize your body becoming a sacred vessel. Imagine that the life force of the earth is flowing up through you, and at the same time, the energy of the heavens above is cascading down upon you.

When you enter into the stillness, there will be messages all around you. Watch for signs. (You might want to have your Process Journal or pen and paper by your side to record any insights.) If you're outdoors, watch the movement of animals, birds, and clouds. If you're indoors, try to position yourself so that you can see out a window. Notice the movement of the clouds or what else occurs outside, but also be aware of signs within your home. *Your body will be giving you signs and messages as well.* For example, if you're sitting in your sacred circle in your home and out of the window you see a cloud that somehow reminds you of your mother—and at the same time you feel a tightening sensation in your stomach area—this could indicate that there's an unresolved issue regarding your mother that has lodged in your abdomen. You may want to then close your eyes and journey to this area in your body in order to converse with the Guardian of your stomach and ask for assistance in resolving the blockage.

Your body communicates messages from Spirit, so pay attention to the physical sensations that occur during your Quest. Your soul will also speak to you during this time, so be aware of every feeling that surfaces. Here are some things you might want to consider doing on your Quest:

- Ask yourself, *If I knew what my body wanted me to know, what would it be?*

- Be aware of your thoughts and the feelings that flow up from your body.

- Delve deep into your body to find the Creator that dwells there.

- Send prayers and blessings to your body.

> **<u>Reward</u>**
> My fabulous reward for completing this
> entire 28-day program is:
>
>
> (Gift yourself this reward at the successful
> completion of today's exercises.)

In powerful and often mysterious ways, the effects
of this program will manifest in your health and vitality
for years to come.

*You have my love and support on your continuing journey
into the secret messages of the body.*
— Denise

><———— ✢ ————<

Acknowledgments

My deepest gratitude to LuAnn Cibik for all that you do for the Soul Coaching® community.

To Allison Harter, for the incredible support you continue to give to me and to Soul Coaching®.

To Louis and Maurica Zimmerman and your wonderful family. I'm deeply honored by the depth of your love.

To my amazingly glorious friend Amber Salisbury, who knows the power of a tiara.

About the Author

Denise Linn is an internationally renowned teacher in the field of self-development. She's the author of the bestseller *Sacred Space* and the award-winning *Feng Shui for the Soul*, and has written 16 books, which are available in 24 languages. Denise has appeared in numerous documentaries and television shows worldwide, gives seminars on six continents, and is the founder of the International Institute of Soul Coaching®, which offers professional certification programs in life coaching and past-life regression. To arrange a session with a Soul Coach to support you on this 28-day program, please visit: **www.Soul-Coaching.com**. For information about Denise's Soul Coaching certification program and other lectures, please visit her Website: **www.DeniseLinn.com**, or write to her at:

Denise Linn Seminars
P.O. Box 759
Paso Robles, California 93447

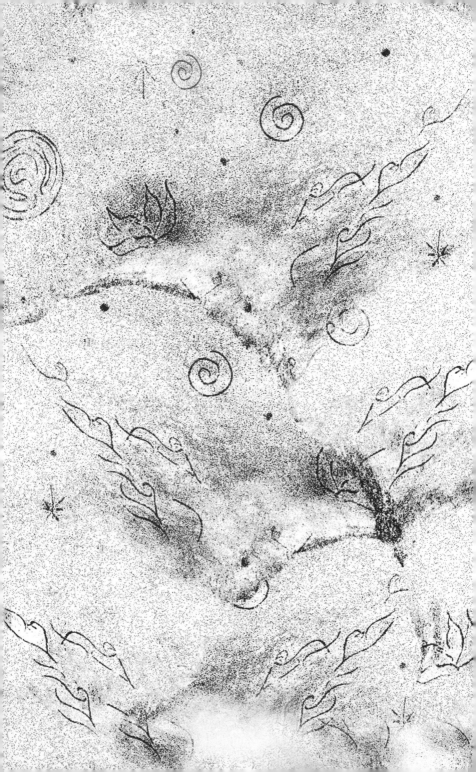

Hay House Titles of Related Interest

YOU CAN HEAL YOUR LIFE, the movie,
starring Louise L. Hay & Friends
(available as a 1-DVD program and
an expanded 2-DVD set)
Watch the trailer at: **www.LouiseHayMovie.com**

THE SHIFT, the movie,
starring Dr. Wayne W. Dyer
(available as a 1-DVD program and
an expanded 2-DVD set)
Watch the trailer at: **www.DyerMovie.com**

✤ ✤ ✤

THE BODY "KNOWS": How to Tune In to Your
Body and Improve Your Health, by Caroline Sutherland

EXCUSES BEGONE! How to Change Lifelong,
Self-Defeating Thinking Habits, by Dr. Wayne W. Dyer

THE FUTURE IS NOW: Timely Advice
for Creating a Better World, by His Holiness
the 17th Gyalwang Karmapa

HEALING YOUR FAMILY HISTORY: 5 Steps to Break Free of Destructive Patterns, Rebecca Linder Hintze

JUICY LIVING, JUICY AGING: Kick Up Your Heels . . . Before You're Too Short to Wear Them, by Loretta LaRoche

THE POWER IS WITHIN YOU, by Louise L. Hay

WHAT IS YOUR SELF-WORTH? A Woman's Guide to Validation, by Cheryl Saban, Ph.D.

All of the above are available at your
local bookstore, or may be ordered
by contacting Hay House.

✿ ✿ ✿

We hope you enjoyed this Hay House book. If you'd like to receive our online catalog featuring additional information on Hay House books and products, or if you'd like to find out more about the Hay Foundation, please contact:

Hay House, Inc., P.O. Box 5100, Carlsbad, CA 92018-5100

(760) 431-7695 or **(800) 654-5126**
(760) 431-6948 (fax) or **(800) 650-5115 (fax)**
www.hayhouse.com® • **www.hayfoundation.org**

✿ ✿ ✿

Published and distributed in Australia by: Hay House Australia Pty. Ltd.,
18/36 Ralph St., Alexandria NSW 2015 • *Phone:* 612-9669-4299
Fax: 612-9669-4144 • www.hayhouse.com.au

Published and distributed in the United Kingdom by: Hay House UK, Ltd.,
292B Kensal Rd., London W10 5BE • *Phone:* 44-20-8962-1230
Fax: 44-20-8962-1239 • www.hayhouse.co.uk

Published and distributed in the Republic of South Africa by: Hay House SA (Pty), Ltd.,
P.O. Box 990, Witkoppen 2068 • *Phone/Fax:* 27-11-467-8904
info@hayhouse.co.za • www.hayhouse.co.za

Published in India by: Hay House Publishers India, Muskaan Complex, Plot No. 3,
B-2, Vasant Kunj, New Delhi 110 070 • *Phone:* 91-11-4176-1620
Fax: 91-11-4176-1630 • www.hayhouse.co.in

Distributed in Canada by: Raincoast, 9050
Shaughnessy St., Vancouver, B.C. V6P 6E5
Phone: (604) 323-7100 • *Fax:* (604) 323-2600 • www.raincoast.com

✿ ✿ ✿

Take Your Soul on a Vacation

Visit **www.HealYourLife.com**® to regroup, recharge, and reconnect
with your own magnificence. Featuring blogs, mind-body-spirit news,
and life-changing wisdom from Louise Hay and friends.

Visit **www.HealYourLife.com** today!

Mind Your Body,
Mend Your Spirit

Hay House is the ultimate resource for inspirational and health-conscious books, audio programs, movies, events, e-newsletters, member communities, and much more.

Visit **www.hayhouse.com**® today and nourish your soul.

UPLIFTING EVENTS

Join your favorite authors at live events in a city near you or log on to **www.hayhouse.com** to visit with Hay House authors online during live, interactive Web events.

INSPIRATIONAL RADIO

Daily inspiration while you're at work or at home. Enjoy radio programs featuring your favorite authors, streaming live on the Internet 24/7 at **HayHouseRadio.com**®. Tune in and tune up your spirit!

VIP STATUS

Join the Hay House VIP membership program today and enjoy exclusive discounts on books, CDs, calendars, card decks, and more. You'll also receive 10% off all event reservations (excluding cruises). Visit **www.hayhouse.com/wisdom** to join the Hay House Wisdom Community™.

Visit **www.hayhouse.com** and enter priority code 2723
during checkout for special savings!
(One coupon per customer.)

HAYHOUSE
RADIO))
radio for your soul™

HAY HOUSE
Wisdom

HEAL YOUR LIFE ♥

Take Your Soul on a Vacation

Get your daily dose of inspiration today at **www.HealYourLife.com®**. Brimming with all of the necessary elements to ease your mind and educate your soul, this Website will become the foundation from which you'll start each day. This essential site delivers the latest in mind, body, and spirit news and real-time content from your favorite Hay House authors.

Make It Your Home Page Today!

www.HealYourLife.com®

www.hayhouse.com®